Thomas Bossius is Lecturer in Cultural Studies at the University of Gothenburg. **Andreas Häger** is Docent in Sociology of Religion at Åbo Akademi University, Turku. **Keith Kahn-Harris** is an Honorary Research Fellow in the Department of Psycho-Social Studies at Birkbeck College, London, and author of *Extreme Metal: Music and Culture on the Edge* (2006).

'Within the growing literature on religion, media and culture, comparatively little attention has been given to popular music, and even less to the ways in which religious groups use popular music to re-negotiate their traditions in the modern world. Drawing on a wide range of well-informed case studies, *Religion and Popular Music in Europe* helps to address this gap, and will be an important resource for tutors, students and researchers.'

Gordon Lynch, Michael Ramsey Professor of Modern Theology,
University of Kent

'*Religion and Popular Music in Europe* is an excellent example of scholarship at the interface of Religious Studies and Popular Music Studies. Its various perspectives provide thought-provoking analysis of the ways in which religions and alternative spiritualities use popular music in their engagement with the modern world. I thoroughly enjoyed reading the book and enthusiastically commend it as a significant contribution to the study of religion and popular music.'

Christopher Partridge, Professor of Religious Studies,
Lancaster University

RELIGION AND POPULAR MUSIC IN EUROPE

New Expressions of Sacred and Secular Identity

Edited by

Thomas Bossius

Andreas Häger & Keith Kahn-Harris

I.B. TAURIS

LONDON · NEW YORK

Published in 2011 by I.B.Tauris & Co Ltd
6 Salem Road, London W2 4BU
175 Fifth Avenue, New York NY 10010
www.ibtauris.com

Distributed in the United States and Canada Exclusively by Palgrave Macmillan
175 Fifth Avenue, New York NY 10010

This book is number 52 in the series Studies on Inter-Religious Relations,
edited by Ingvar Svanberg and David Westerlund, and is contiguously
number 18 in the I.B.Tauris Library of Modern Religion series.

Library of Modern Religion, Vol 18

ISBN: 978 1 84885 809 1

A full CIP record for this book is available from the British Library
A full CIP record is available from the Library of Congress

Library of Congress Catalog Card Number: available

Printed and bound in Great Britain by CPI Antony Rowe, Chippenham

Contents

Acknowledgements

This book has been a few years in the making. During these years, the work has involved several people, to which we would like to extend our thanks. First of all we would like to thank Professor David Westerlund at Södertörn University, for his invaluable help financially as well as practically. With funding from his and Ingvar Svanberg's book series 'Studies on Inter-Religious Relations', David Westerlund financed the language revision and helped us with the printing costs for the book. Professor Ove Sernhede and Dr Catharina Thörn at the Forum for Studies of Contemporary Culture (FSSK) at the University of Gothenburg funded an initial meeting in Gothenburg, and also helped us by contributing to the financing of the printing of the book. A special thank you goes to Everett Thiele for the language revision, and Elisabeth Sandberg for making the index. We would also like to thank Mercedes Carpintero, Ayhan Erol, Lina Molokotos-Liederman, Stella Sai-Chun Lau and Graham St. John, who initially were part of this book project, but who, for different reasons, were not involved in production of the book. Finally we would like to thank I.B. Tauris and especially our senior editor Alex Wright and our production editor Victoria Nemeth, also Carolann Martin at Initial Typesetting Services for good and friendly cooperation.

Introduction

Religion and popular music in Europe

Thomas Bossius,
Keith Kahn-Harris
& Andreas Häger

Throughout human history music and religion have walked hand in hand. In rites and rituals in small tribal religions, in the great world religions, and in the contemporary New Age, neo-pagan and neo-heathen movements, different kinds of music are used to celebrate the gods, to express beliefs, and to help believers to get in contact with the divine.

This book focuses on how organised, mainstream religious groups, as well as counter-cultural or subcultural groups, use religion and music to negotiate the problems of modernisation, religious change and globalisation. Since the days of the hippie movement of the late 1960s and early 1970s, popular music has been a field where existential questions, ideology and religion have been negotiated and expressed. Among organised, mainstream religious groups popular music is used to express, discuss and spread their beliefs. This is true of world religions such as Islam, Judaism, Hinduism and Christianity, as well as new religious groups such as the Hare Krishna and the New Age movements. Most well known and successful is the popular music of Christianity, usually called Contemporary Christian Music (CCM). Religion has also been an important (and all too frequently, critically neglected) element in a wide range of popular music cultures. Religion and popular music interact and cross-fertilise in genres such as reggae with its connections to the Rastafari religion; black metal with strong connections to neo-paganism and Satanism; and psychedelic trance where 'hippie religion', New Age, neo-shamanism and neo-paganism play important roles.

All these groups and movements have taken on a renewed importance in contemporary Europe. Europe is undergoing a process of rapid
change in which internal ethnic diversity is more recognised than ever,
and in which the borders of Europe continue to expand with the entry
of new states into the EU. Such rapid change has led inevitably to
tensions and conflict. Religion provides a powerful way for individuals
to find community, identity and security in a rapidly changing world.
Religious groups are ever more implicated in a process of increasing
European differentiation. Music provides a way in which this conflict
and change can be responded to and negotiated. Controversies over
music are often the 'lightning rod' for serious debates about the nature
of religious identity and practice. The prominence and importance of
such debates has continued to grow since the 1950s with the rise to
global prominence of originally African American forms of popular
music. Rock, pop and dance music in their multifarious forms are
variously constructed as symbols of the corruption of secular society,
as resources for new forms of worship and religious identification, and
as ways of attracting new adherents and followers. Investigating the
relationship between European religious groups and contemporary
forms of popular music opens a window onto the strains, stresses and
potentials of contemporary religion. In an attempt to open this window
Religion and Popular Music in Europe addresses the question: how do the
people of contemporary Europe use popular music to negotiate religious
change and conflict, and what functions does popular music fill for
them in this process?

Much of the published research on religion and popular music
focuses on the Anglo-Saxon and above all the American context (e.g.
Spencer 1994; Gilmour 2005). This anthology tries to balance this
emphasis by focusing on Europe and including cases from various non-
English-speaking societies. Although some of the chapters in the book,
perhaps most obviously the ones dealing with Christianity, do show similarities with North American religion and popular music, other cases, for
example the discussions of black metal and French rap music, emphasise
the specificity of local contexts of religion and popular music in Europe.

The book

'Popular Music', 'Religion' and indeed 'Europe' are all slippery concepts, used in different ways by different people for different purposes. Religion can refer both to a bounded and specific set of institutions and practices that endure over time and to a more nebulous sense of the spiritual as it interpenetrates with everyday life. In this book we are principally interested in the former definition of religion, particularly the organised practices of the three monotheistic religions, but in our final chapters we do include two cases of the latter to provide a point of comparison. Music has in most places and times been associated with religious practices, both in elitist ways (as produced for example by priestly castes) and in ways that are quite literally popular in the sense of being produced and listened to by the masses. For the purposes of this book we define popular music fairly narrowly as that which owes something – musically, semiotically and sociologically – to the musical cultures that emerged out of black America in the 1950s; in other words, rock and roll and its descendants. We are most interested, then, in how post-1950s popular music relates to the major world religions.

We see Europe as a space that, while centred on the EU and 'old Europe', has become much more flexible and undefined in recent years. In a globalised world, nation-states and geographical regions cannot be seen as bounded and autonomous. States such as Turkey exist in an ambivalent space that is both European and something else. Further, 'the global' intersects with the local in myriad complex ways. This is particularly true in the case of religion and popular music, as both are spheres of activity in which communities are interlinked with one another across the globe. Muslims in Europe are part of a global *umah* that influences the nature of local Muslim interaction, both musically and otherwise. Similarly, Christian and Jewish popular music scenes in Europe, like their secular equivalents, are inextricably tied into global scenes.

This book focuses on four religious spaces and their relationship to popular music: Christianity, Judaism, Islam and New Religious Movements.

Christianity

In the Christian church music has always been an important part of the liturgy. The early church inherited and reworked the rich musical heritage of Judaism. The purpose and ideology behind the earliest songs seems to have been simply that they were for the benefit of the congregation as a means of spiritual edification. However, even during the first centuries of Christianity the church fathers discussed not only how music could best be forged into the life of the church and used as an edificatory tool, but also how it could be used to win unbelievers over to Christianity. The early church was opposed to instrumental music and the use of instruments as an accompaniment to singing, because it was felt that instrumental music, instead of turning heathens towards Christ, turned Christians towards heathen temptations (Benestad 1994/1978: 41–48; Grout 1978: 11–27). This kind of thinking about music is still evident in some contemporary Christian churches and movements.

Since the late 1800s, when the Salvation Army started putting Christian lyrics to secular melodies, popular music has been widely used in Protestant churches. This music differs considerably from the music of the early church, but the starting point and justification for the use of music is practically the same as before. Howard and Streck (1999) speak of three different rationales for using popular music within Christianity and particularly in the form of CCM. The first is the use of popular music as a means of evangelisation, reaching out to people outside the congregation. Later, as it became evident that the music was not reaching out as effectively as expected, the main reason for using the music was to provide alternative, 'safe' entertainment for Christian youth. A third and more recent rationale for CCM, according to Howard and Streck (1999) is to see it as art for its own sake.

Thomas Bossius's chapter focuses on the development of Christian worship music (CWM) within the European evangelical Christian movements of the late twentieth and early twenty-first centuries. Beginning in the 1970s, CWM developed into one of the dominant genres in the contemporary Christian music scene. Worship music took a central position among young Christians, influencing church music and engendering an associated lifestyle. At worship services and concerts, traditional elements of the church services are mixed with elements from the concert culture of popular music. CWM positions itself in a liminal space between popular and church culture.

Marcus Moberg's chapter highlights the internationally growing Christian metal scene with the focus on developments in Finland. Christian metal crosses over all three of the rationales pointed out by Howard and Streck (1999). It started out as a means of evangelisation, but immediately also acquired the role of a 'safe entertainment alternative' for young Christians. It is a good example of how Christianity is dealing with the problems of secularisation and religious change, but also of how music is used as art for its own sake, and as an alternative youth culture within evangelical Christianity.

Although most kinds of popular music are widely accepted in contemporary Christianity, the chapter by Andreas Häger provides an example of how some kinds of music still can be seen as controversial. Häger's case study is the Swedish Christian hard rock group Jerusalem and its relationship to the neo-Pentecostal 'Livets Ord' ('Word of Life') congregation of Uppsala, Sweden. Jerusalem, founded in 1975, were pioneers of Christian heavy rock, and are considered to be among the founding fathers of Christian heavy metal. From 1985 to 1992 the (then) members, including the leader and lead singer Ulf Christiansson, belonged to and were closely tied to Livets Ord. This chapter looks at various representations of Jerusalem's time in the Uppsala congregation, and what their presence as a well-known rock group meant for Livets Ord. The aim is to gain an understanding not only of a period of the career of a Christian rock group, but of the significance of rock music in a congregation like Livets Ord, and of the relationship between this type of Christianity and Swedish society.

Judaism

Judaism has a long musical tradition that is as complex as the Christian tradition. To be a Jew is not simply to have faith in a particular religious tradition but also to identify with a particular conception of peoplehood. As such, Jewishness does not conform to simple understandings of religion as spiritual practice, but intersects with concepts such as 'ethnicity' and 'nation'. Jewishness can be articulated through practices that might be defined as 'secular' in their lack of spiritual or ritualistic reference. Throughout much of Jewish history, and even today, the division between the religious and the secular has been blurred within Jewish practice. In modern times, however, the possibilities to differentiate between secular and religious Jewish practices have become greater. The seeds of this potential bifurcation were already present in the early history of Jewish music. For example, the prohibition against instrumental music on the Sabbath and most religious festivals created the possibility for distinctive types of Jewish instrumental music to be developed for weddings and other occasions with a weaker religious element. In modernity, the development of explicitly and implicitly secular forms of Jewish identification has meant that some genres of Jewish music such as klezmer have been treated as vehicles for the development of a non-religious form of Jewish music (Slobin 2000). Moreover, non-religious, assimilated Jews have been heavily involved in the creation of post-war Anglo-American popular music in ways that may be highly distinctive, but are generally non-religious (see for example Melnik 2001). At the same time, the complexities of Jewish identity are such that it can be difficult to tell where the ethnic ends and the religious starts in Jewish music.

The consequences of the complex relationship between secular and religious forms of Jewishness can be seen in a consideration of contemporary Jewish liturgical music. Keith Kahn-Harris's chapter looks at how one particular form of popular music – 'Contemporary Jewish Music' – has drawn on forms of contemporary popular music in ways that are analogous to the development of Contemporary Christian Music. Kahn-Harris shows how this music has circulated between the British and American Jewish communities. In particular he looks at how the music of the pioneering contemporary American Jewish musician Debbie Friedman has been received in Britain. He discusses how contemporary Jewish music both provides a cultural 'bridge' between two Jewish communities, and also highlights deep differences between them. The chapter argues that an examination of the interaction of popular music and religion sheds light on the interplay between the two forces of global fragmentation and unification. By looking at how religious communities in one location draw on popular music from another location, we gain insight into the ways in which religion is positioned in relation to global cultural flows.

Islam

Islam offers a rich variety of religious music, from the sung call for prayer, Koran recitations, hymns and other ritual music, to the advanced art music of Sufi mysticism (Hjärpe 2001: 56). Just as in Christianity, there is a lively discussion within Islam about the role and function of music, and about what kinds of music are acceptable and can be useful. Hjärpe writes that the attitudes towards music waver between the approaches 'recommended, allowed, forbidden' (Hjärpe 2001: 57). Certain forms of Islamic music have reached far outside its own cultural sphere, and become part of the global popular music scene, such as the work of the Pakistani qawalli musician Nusrat Fateh Ali Khan. Strong influences from Islam can also be found in the hip hop culture of many Western countries. In this book Stéphanie Molinero covers this aspect with her chapter on the French hip hop scene.

In his chapter Göran Larsson looks at musical thinking and negotiations of Islam in general, and in the work of Yusuf Islam (formerly known as Cat Stevens) in particular. With his conversion to Islam in 1977 Cat Stevens gave up his stardom, abandoned the music industry and changed his name to Yusuf Islam. Although his conversion to Islam was not conditional on his abandonment of music, he turned his back on the music industry for almost three decades. With the 2006 release of the album *An Other Cup* Yusuf Islam returned to the music scene. His decision to leave the business was based on his conviction that the music industry had a destructive side that was not good for him. The decision to quit recording music and stop performing live concerts was ultimately his own. With the release of *An Other Cup* his opinion on music had clearly changed. Larsson's chapter casts light on how this change came about. As a foundation for his discussion of Yusuf Islam's opinion on music, Larsson also gives a brief overview of the discussion about music in Islamic theology and history.

New Religious Movements

In contemporary Western society where Christianity has lost much of its former status and authority, religion continues – in other forms and shapes, and often in an intimate harmony with music – to fill important functions for many people. Sociological studies on young people and religion during the past few decades have shown that a relatively large proportion of young people studied see music as something holy and spiritual (Sjödin 2001; Bossius 2003). Music is associated with religion, and musical experiences are described as religious experiences. Sometimes this connection is developed into subcultural practices where music and religion are used in a complex way to negotiate the problems of contemporary society.

In addition to popular music being seen as religious in often vague terms, popular music culture has often provided the motivating factor and/or central organising principle behind the development of what are sometimes called New Religious Movements. Gry Mørk's chapter focuses on neo-Paganism and its relationship to Norwegian black metal, and its struggle against what it considers to be the hegemony of the Christian state religion. In 1993 the Norwegian media publicised the extraordinary activities of the black metal scene. Members of the Norwegian black metal scene had engaged in criminal activities including arson attacks on churches, desecration of graves, assault and battery, and even murder. These criminal acts, the generally violent profile of the scene, and the musical style of black metal, led to claims that Norway was confronting a satanic and destructive movement that was undermining society. Despite the secularisation and individualism characteristic of Norway, Christian discourses still pervade some sectors of society such as the judicial and educational systems. Black metal is on many levels deeply concerned with individuation and differentiation, and because of this it is an expression of the opposition between the individual and the predominant social system.

Rupert Till's chapter explores the relationships between Electronic Dance Music Culture (EDMC) and trance, religion, meaning and spirituality. EDMC covers a coherent group of activities and cultural practices, including those in some nightclubs, at free parties and festivals, and focuses on music genres such as trance, techno, house and drum and bass, while excluding mainstream chart music, rap and hip hop. Till's work is focused principally on England, although it resonates with and relates to EDMC worldwide. Overt religious references are most common within the trance music sub-genre, and it is the trance music scene that Till focuses on, although elements of religion and spirituality pervade EDMC in general to some extent. Clubbing has been shown to be meaningful for participants and in a sense performs a religious function, and clubbers are parts of neo-tribes, making fearless leaps into uncertainty. EDMC is related to religious festivals, or celebration, and can be regarded as implicit religion. It exhibits many features of New Religious Movements, demonstrates socio-cultural revitalisation, and is highly meaningful and transformative. It is clear that for those involved in EDMC it fulfils many of the functions traditionally served by religions, and that it bears many of the hallmarks and typical features of religion and spirituality.

About the authors

Religion and Popular Music is a collaboration between eight scholars from five different European countries: Sweden, Norway, Finland, Great Britain and France. The authors are presented here in alphabetical order:

Thomas Bossius is a Lecturer and Researcher in Cultural Studies at the Department of Cultural Sciences at the University of Gothenburg. He received a PhD in musicology in 2003. His dissertation was a study of the interactive use of music and religion in black metal and psychedelic trance culture. His ongoing main research focus is the interaction between popular music and religion. Together with Andreas Häger, he has initiated a study on Christian Popular Music. He has also completed studies of drug use at music festivals and in the club culture of contemporary Sweden. He is now working on a study on the functions of music in everyday life together with Lars Lilliestam, professor of musicology at the University of Gothenburg.

Andreas Häger is Docent in Sociology of Religion at Åbo Akademi University, Turku (Åbo), Finland. Häger received his PhD in the sociology of religion from Uppsala University, Uppsala, Sweden, in 2001. The thesis was a study of Christian discourses on popular music. Häger's post-doctoral research focuses on contemporary Christian music as well as on religious features of mainstream popular music.

Keith Kahn-Harris is a research associate at the Centre for Urban and Community Research, Goldsmiths College, London. He completed his PhD at the same institution in 2001. He is the author of *Extreme Metal: Music and Culture on the Edge* (Berg 2006) and co-editor (with Andrew Bennett) of *After Subculture: Critical Studies in Contemporary Youth Culture* (Palgrave 2004). He is also the convener of *New Jewish Thought* (www.newjewishthought.org).

Göran Larsson is Senior Lecturer and post-doctoral researcher in the Swedish national research programme LearnIT, funded by the Knowledge Foundation. He earned his PhD in religious studies at the University of Gothenburg, Sweden, in 2000. He has published several articles and books on Muslims in the West (both past and present), Quranic studies, media and religion, youth culture and religion in Swedish and English. His book *Ibn García's shu'ubiyya Letter: Ethnic and Theological Tensions in Medieval al-Andalus* was published by Brill Academic Press in 2003.

Marcus Moberg is a post-doctoral researcher at the Department of Comparative Religion at Åbo Akademi University, Turku (Åbo), Finland. He defended his doctoral thesis on the Finnish and transnational Christian metal music scene in 2009. He is currently working within the project *Post-secular Culture and a Changing Religious Landscape in Finland* (PCCR) at Åbo Akademi University.

Stéphanie Molinero received her PhD in sociology in 2007 at the University of Franche-Comté, Paris. In her thesis, she analyses the different types of reception of rap in France, and of flamenco in Spain. She teaches sociology at the University of Vincennes-Paris 8.

Gry Mørk received a master's degree in religious studies at the University of Tromsø in 2002. Her master's thesis *Drømmer om fortiden, minner for fremtiden* ('Dreams of the Past, Memories for the Future'; 2002) covers the pagan/Viking/nationalist perspectives of Norwegian black metal in its initial phase from 1992 to 1995.

Rupert Till is senior lecturer at the University of Huddersfield, England, where he teaches music, music technology and popular music. He is active as a composer and performer of electronic and acoustic ambient music, having studied composition with Gavin Bryars and Katharine Norman, amongst others. The main focus of his research is the musicological study of popular music, with publications that focus on Electronic Dance Music, as well as music, religion and spirituality. He is also carrying out research on the acoustics and music of British neolithic archaeological sites, including Stonehenge.

1

Jerusalem in Uppsala

Some accounts of the relationship between a Christian rock group and its congregation

Andreas Häger

Introduction

The Swedish Christian hard rock group Jerusalem was founded in Gothenburg, Sweden, in 1975.[1] Their first record was released three years later, and the band's official website informs us:

> The record 'Jerusalem' became an instant hit among the Christian audience. In the first six months the record sold 20 000 copies.

The group quickly became famous as a touring group, also touring outside of Sweden.[2] A few years later they were touring in North America and their videos were being played on America's MTV channel. The history on the website continues:

> Eventually it all became too much. Jerusalem pulled the emergency brake. The glamorous life had become too much. The band was tired. In 1985, Jerusalem quit touring. They moved with their families to Uppsala and went to Word of Life Bible school. A new journey began, where the music had to stand back. Jesus was put first.

The band stayed in Uppsala until 1993.[3] This chapter deals with

Jerusalem's time in the 'Livets Ord' (in English 'Word of Life') con-gregation[4] in Uppsala. The goal of this chapter is to study various 'representations' or descriptions of this time, and what it meant to the group, its fans, and to the congregation.

The Livets Ord congregation can be described as neo-Pentecostal, with an emphasis on 'faith' (or 'prosperity') teaching, and it has a strong reputation for being in conflict with the surrounding society, includ-ing other Christians (Coleman 1991).[5] As I will illustrate with some examples in this chapter, one aspect of this conflict has been a harsh criticism of the popular cultural expression of rock music. The presence of a well-known Christian hard rock group in this congregation – and its departure from the congregation – is therefore in itself an interesting occurrence.

From a theoretical perspective, the discussion here attempts to go beyond a mere description of this interesting occurrence and view the relation of Livets Ord to rock music as an example of how a particular religious organisation deals with the modern culture of the surrounding society. The main theoretical starting point used here for such a discus-sion is the concept of religious legitimation, as presented by Berger (1967) and Berger and Luckmann (1971/1966). I see the discussion on rock music and the role of rock music as part of the legitimation – or in some cases de-legitimation – of Livets Ord. A possible consequence of such a perspective, and one that I have discussed at greater length elsewhere (Häger 2001), is to understand rock music, and contemporary culture in general, as a competitor in the field of world views. The dis-cussion on the role of rock music in an organisation such as Livets Ord, or within Christianity in general, can then be seen as the defence of a position, a perceived monopoly, in the field of world views. This defence is always a question of balance: what can be allowed or even used for one's own purposes, as in the case of Christian rock, and what must be forbidden? A central aspect of this precarious balance is the construction of dichotomies: us/them, good/bad, divine/demonic, etc. In the presenta-tion of documents on Jerusalem's time as members of Livets Ord, I give here examples of how such a balance is attempted, and how precarious it may be – how the line is drawn, and then drawn again somewhere else.

Another central theoretical concept is the concept of representa-tion. This concept is borrowed from Stuart Hall (1997), and here it denotes above all that the image or account of a certain event or phenomenon is not a reflection of the object it represents but part of the construction of the object. The various descriptions of Jerusalem's time in Livets Ord are representations[6] that are part of the social construction of reality – of what 'really' happened, and what it meant to Jerusalem in particular and for rock music in general at Livets Ord at the time in question. They are therefore part of the struggle over the legitimacy of the organisation.

The starting point of this chapter is a piece of empirical data: the members of a certain rock group spent some time in a particular Christian congregation. The main content will also be the presentation and re-presentation of different empirical materials relating to this initial observation. The task at hand is, however, not to find out what happened, but rather to see how different sources describe and interpret the role of the rock group Jerusalem during its time in Uppsala. This is particularly valid in the part of the chapter that deals with a situation of conflict where very different perspectives are expressed by the various participants. The difference in the representations is understood as an indication of the complexity of the relation between a religious organ-isation such as Livets Ord – traditionally referred to in the sociology of religion as a 'sect' type of organisation – and contemporary culture, here exemplified by rock music.

Most of the material used is unprompted or 'spontaneous' in the sense that it has come into existence without the researcher's inter-vention. The exceptions are two interviews; most importantly one with a former Livets Ord member, here nicknamed 'Håkan' (Håkan 1999), who was a member of Livets Ord at roughly the same time as Jerusalem. The unprompted part of the material consists of articles from two magazines, *Magazinet* and *Trons Värld*; taped sermons with the leader of Livets Ord, pastor Ulf Ekman; records and a video by the group Jerusalem; and the group's official website. *Magazinet* was the official Livets Ord periodical, with editorials by Ulf Ekman, other longer opinion pieces as well as longer features. *Trons Värld* is relatively independent, yet at the time was closely associated to Livets Ord, as a privately owned magazine started and run entirely by (then) members of the congregation and dedicated to covering issues of interest to the neopentecostal faith/prosperity movement (Holmström 1996: 124–36;

Interview with Krister Holmström). *Trons Värld* is more news oriented than *Magazinet*, with a regular music section including interviews, reports and reviews. Part of the material was produced during the period under study, but some was produced after 1993, and views the period in hindsight. The band's website, together with the interview with Håkan, make up the most important post-1993 material. Quotations are given in my translation from Swedish, except for song titles and lyrics by Jerusalem and the biographical and band-history website material which is published in English.

Some of the material on the group's website consists of answers given by Jerusalem's leader and lead singer Ulf Christiansson to questions mailed in by fans. Therefore, the option existed for me to do the same and email questions directly to the group and its leader. I have however elected to forego such an opportunity. One reason for this is that Christiansson has been very reluctant to comment on the Livets Ord period (see below); another reason is that I am trying to collect various images or representations of the period studied, and there is a great risk that any form of interview with the group's lead singer could be perceived – by myself and others – as the definitive account of the group's time in Livets Ord. This would not the serve the aim of this chapter.

The presentation of the material is primarily chronological, in the sense that the next section of the chapter deals with Jerusalem's time in Livets Ord, and the following section deals with their departure from Uppsala. That section also discusses some background material not directly linked to Jerusalem but concerning Livets Ord's views on rock music in general instead. The chapter concludes with a short discussion.

Jerusalem in Uppsala

This section presents a perspective on the position of Jerusalem (and its lead singer Ulf Christiansson) in Livets Ord in the late 1980s, and briefly discusses the role of music in Livets Ord in general and music as a means of 'spiritual warfare'.

The very first issue of *Trons Värld* in 1988 contains an article on a concert tour by Jerusalem in central Europe, with a picture of the lead singer Ulf Christiansson on the cover, and a whole spread devoted to the band. This attention to the group in the very first issue of the magazine can be taken as an indication that the group played an important role in the congregation and (thus) in the whole of the Swedish faith movement at the time.[7] The group, and particularly their lead singer, was featured regularly in both *Trons Värld* and *Magazinet* during their time in Uppsala. There are interviews with Ulf Christiansson (*Magazinet* 1990a: 10–12) and even articles by him (*Magazinet* 1989a: 42–43) in the congregation's official publication, as well as many reports on the group's tours – with an emphasis on the number of people converted at different concerts – in the more news-oriented sections of *Trons Värld* (e.g. 1988a: 15; 1988b: 20), with headlines such as '50 saved on Jerusalem tour' (*Trons Värld* 1988c: 20). Ulf Christiansson also preached at meetings in the congregation, including some of the major conferences (see e.g. *Trons Värld* 1990a: 19).

As previously mentioned, the relationship between Livets Ord and the surrounding society has been characterised by tension. The congregation has been much criticised both by other Christian organisations and secular circles (Coleman 1991). This criticism, sometimes bordering on hostility, has according to sources within the congregation also affected Jerusalem, when there was a bomb threat against a concert in Uppsala that had to be postponed (*Trons Värld* 1990c: 13). One of the pastors of Livets Ord is quoted as saying 'the Jerusalem concert wasn't the only meeting to be threatened by bombs' (ibid.). The concert was part of a larger event called 'Jesus festival', arranged by the congregation, which in itself indicates that the rock music of Jerusalem was an integral part of the congregation's activities. The group and its music are further defined by the quoted pastor as part of the congregation both when he calls the concert a 'meeting' (in Swedish 'möte'), a word used for religious gatherings, and when he emphasises that the group was the object of opposition by people outside the congregation, as were other aspects of the congregation's activities during the same festival.

A bomb had exploded in the congregation's facilities a few weeks earlier (*Dagens Nyheter* 1990), and this festival also received bomb threats. The threats of physical violence are used to emphasise the degree of conflict with and separation from secular society, and they therefore reinforce the sense of being unique and chosen that was felt by Livets Ord and Jerusalem. In short, the comments on the bomb threats become part of the legitimation of Livets Ord, and of Jerusalem's position in the congregation at the time.

Music is important in Livets Ord, as can be seen from the material considered here. The two magazines already discussed, particularly *Trons Värld*, devote substantial space to music, with interviews, reviews and articles looking at music from a Christian perspective.[8] The next section looks more closely at the debates on music and rock music in particular. But here the focus is on the central role of music in the religious practice of the congregation, in the services.[9]

In my interview with former Livets Ord member Håkan he tells of the significance of music to his Christian life. He liked modern music, and chose to become active in the faith movement because of this. He explained that 'after a while I became more involved in the faith movement and there was a great acceptance of rock music'.

Håkan continued:

> the music played an important role in Livets Ord. As I experienced it, this was what meant the most to me as a member of Livets Ord. I went to the services because of this music, really, and my encounter with God was actually . . . so to speak, standing there and singing with the music.

Håkan joined the Livets Ord Bible school in the mid-1980s:

> I must say that the Livets Ord youth meetings, they were something special. Saturday nights there were meetings with the same praise songs that I was used to from meetings [at home] but they had some kind of hard rock band playing and high volume and quite a lot of energy – it was rock.

He added that the members of Jerusalem sometimes played in the praise rock band during these Saturday night meetings, that distortion was used on the guitar and guitar solos were played: 'It was a pretty fantastic emotional and religious experience to celebrate a divine service with distorted guitar, it influenced me very deeply.'

The members of Jerusalem were thus active as musicians in the congregation, and they also continued to do some recording. Jerusalem released one album during their years in Uppsala: *Dancing on the Head of the Serpent* (Jerusalem 1987). The title apparently refers to Genesis

3:15, which talks of the woman's offspring trampling on the serpent's – traditionally interpreted as the devil's – head. The Jerusalem album is described in the website's band-history in the following terms:

> Then as a reaction to the growing Satanism of the 80's they made the record 'Dancing on the head of the Serpent' in 1987 . . . On the sleeve there was an army boot, trampling on a demon. This shocked the Swedish Christianity. The record stores sold the record under the counter.

The album includes, apart from the title track, songs with titles such as 'Plunder hell and populate heaven' and 'Catch the Devil, Catch the Thief'. An attitude of 'spiritual warfare' permeates the record, in accordance with the above-stated purpose of being 'a reaction to the growing Satanism'. Pointing out that the album was sold 'under the counter' in Christian bookstores in Sweden – apparently because of the disturbing image on the cover[10] – can be seen as emphasising their separation from contemporary society: Jerusalem are so completely different that they shock the rest of Swedish Christianity, the majority of whose members affirm modern society, including rock music.

The dualistic, 'spiritual' interpretation of society and culture evident on *Dancing on the Head of the Serpent* was important to Livets Ord at the time, and was also applied to music (e.g. Arnroth 1991: 14–20; Ekman 1993a). Music is seen as spiritual, and therefore permeated either by the holy spirit or by evil spirits – with no possible neutral ground. The fact that music was looked at from the perspective of an important theological standpoint indicates that music was an important phenomenon, and the tendency of Jerusalem to employ the same theology in their lyrics shows that theologically they were a part of the Livets Ord congregation and the faith movement.

In the previously mentioned cover article of the first issue of the magazine *Trons Värld* (1988a: 14–15), the 'spiritual warfare' perspective is also emphasised. The report from a European tour by Jerusalem tells us that a concert was planned with the legendary hard rock group Black Sabbath, but was cancelled on the initiative of Black Sabbath. Christiansson comments on the cancellation, saying:

> It would have been an unparallelled spiritual duel on a rock stage – 'the fathers of Satan's rock' against 'the fathers of

Christian rock'. The victory was of course already decided 2000 years ago on Calvary, but as I said, this time it never came to a fight ... Satan gave a walkover, in other words. (*Trons Värld* 1988a: 14–15)

The cancelled concert is not interpreted as just a rock concert, or as a possibility for an interesting collaboration, but as a 'spiritual duel' and a fight against Satan – a fight that is seen as won in advance. The contrast presented in the repetition of the formula 'fathers of' Christian rock and 'Satan's rock' respectively is a very clear example of the presentation of very sharp dichotomies.

A major theme in the discussion on music at Livets Ord during the period seems to have been the concept of a 'music from heaven', which was expected to be given to the congregation and particularly to Christiansson. This is mentioned in different articles, including interviews with Jerusalem's lead singer. An indication of the prominence of the topic is given when Christiansson says: 'There has been talk of a "Music from heaven" for so long that it now is time for something to come forth' (*Magazinet* 1990a: 11).

Håkan expresses similar feelings:

There was an expectation of this music that Ulf Christiansson promised would come ... we understood from his way of talking that he was promising that some kind of hard rock music would come from heaven that would be, so to speak, completely accepted and pure and cool at the same time, but that music never came.

The expectation of a music from heaven which was to be given to the congregation is perhaps the best example of how music was seen as something spiritual and supernatural, and that the music of this world was believed not to contain the spirit of God. This belief is discussed in the following section.

A new policy on Christian rock

As stated above, music was and is an important issue in Livets Ord, and this is also true of rock music. *Trons Värld* magazine has featured many articles criticising secular rock (see Häger 2001 for a closer discussion), and the Trons Värld press published a book on the topic (Arnroth 1991), with a preface by Ulf Christiansson of Jerusalem. But the attitude to Christian rock was more ambivalent. Christian rock gained a great deal of acceptance as Jerusalem performed at concerts arranged by the congregation, as did other Christian hard rock groups, notably the American group Petra. They received positive media attention (e.g. *Trons Värld* 1990e: 18) and (according to Håkan) had a considerable following among the younger members of the congregation. But Christian rock also came in for criticism, particularly for sounding and looking too much like secular rock (e.g. *Trons Värld* 1988a: 23; 1990d: 18–19).

At one point this criticism of Christian rock, and particularly the type of Christian hard rock represented by groups such as Jerusalem, seems to have rather suddenly become both harsher and much more prominent. This change in policy is to me the most interesting and most challenging aspect of this case, and my main motivation for taking a closer look at this material. In the remainder of this chapter, the difference between the various representations of what happened at this time will be more evident. This section also discusses some background material not directly linked to Jerusalem but relevant to the views on rock music in general.

The (to my knowledge) first documented sign of this change in policy towards rock music at Livets Ord is a sermon by the (then) leader of the congregation, pastor Ulf Ekman, on the 'cassette tape of the month' (of a type that was sent out every month to subscribers) of December 1992. The tape also forms part of a collection of five tapes with sermons by Ulf Ekman, released the following spring under the title *Musikens återupprättelse – Din andliga tempeltjänst inför Gud* (roughly translates as 'The Restoration of Music – Your Spiritual Temple Service before God') (Ekman 1993a). The tapes were apparently recorded at meetings and at the Bible school over a fairly short period in November 1992.[11] The tape of the month of December 1992 was apparently recorded at a youth meeting (which Håkan told me he attended). These tapes contain much interesting material, a few examples of which are considered here. The important point is that they mark an obvious change, and that they contain harsh criticism of Christian rock.

Ekman (1993a) talks of the Old Testament account (in 2. Kings 9) of Jehu and Jezebel and says:

> The Holy Spirit said this to me: Jezebel has come and corrupted many Christian youth through so-called Christian rock music. The time has come when Jehu will make sure that Jezebel lies dead on the plains of Jezreel and the dogs will eat her. This is what the Holy Spirit says in relation to worldly, secularised so-called Christian rock, which is born in rebellion, which actually glorifies sin, which exalts the ego and strikes against anointment.

Christian rock is here identified with one of the least favourably portrayed characters in the Bible, the Baal worshipper Jezebel. It is not as explicit but still possible to presume that Ekman identifies himself with or assumes the role of Jezebel's nemesis, king Jehu.

The key quote in the five tapes is a rhetorical question posed by Ekman (1993a) as a comment on the concept of 'Christian rock'. He says 'There is no such thing as Christian rock. Is there such a thing as Christian sin?'

The concept of Christian rock is presented as a complete oxymoron, and rock music is equated with sin. Ekman recommends that the listeners get rid of their rock records, and particularly mentions the American Christian hard rock group Petra – which (as mentioned above) had been presented as a positive example in *Trons Värld* just two years earlier, and was popular in the congregation. The boundary between good and bad has shifted, and Christian rock music that had been defined as good was now defined as bad.

In order to emphasise that the dichotomy still exists, and that there still can be no confusion as to what is good and what is bad, the dichotomy has to be reinforced even more strongly when the boundary is moved.

Rock music is then defined as fundamentally evil, even in the form of Christian rock. But it must also be noted that in spite of this criticism, contemporary musical instruments, such as drums and electric guitars, were still used at Livets Ord during the mid 1990s. This is audible for example on the record *Låt elden brinna*, which was released by Livets Ord in 1996. The instruments in themselves were not bad.

'Rock' was not primarily associated with contemporary instruments and their sound, but rather with a rebellious attitude or a secular lifestyle, as discussed further below.

Ekman (1993a) also discusses the role of the musicians in the congregation:

> The devil has planned to fill the church[12] with secularised, rebellious musicians that all young people look up to, so that the devil can gain entrance and get the youth to follow him instead of following the living God . . . God has not anointed musicians to lead God's church, but if you ask most young people who they would rather listen to, their pastor or Petra . . .

Ekman does not answer the question. Instead, he interrupts himself and goes on to tell the audience that he has found out that a Petra song, 'God gave rock'n'roll to you', has also been recorded by the secular rock group Kiss (whose music in the Christian anti-rock discourse often is perceived as demonic rock [see Häger 1997 for more on Kiss]). It seems rather clear, though, that Ekman thinks the pastor is the one to lead the congregation and have the ear of the youth, rather than Petra or other rock musicians.

At the beginning of the sermon released as the tape of the month in December 1992, Ekman recounts his perception of the fall of the devil (based on an interpretation of Isaiah 14:11). He tells the audience that the devil had been the song-leader in heaven before the fall, and 'God was like his pastor, if you put it that way'. Ekman (1993b) is very explicit when accusing rock music of being rebellious, and linking the rebellion of rock to the rebellion of the devil. In this quote, he goes beyond equating rock with the devil and also puts the pastor – that is, in the case of the Livets Ord congregation, himself – in the position of God, the one against whom there is a rebellion. Ekman uses this very strong metaphor to legitimate his own position, and the position of the congregation he leads.

The condemnation of Christian rock music expressed by Ekman (1993a) was echoed in Arnroth (1993), in a special issue of *Magazinet* (1993a), and also in articles in *Trons Värld* (e.g. 1993a: 16). This appearance of harsh criticism of a musical style that had previously been accepted was a central theme of my interview with Håkan. Håkan was a great fan of Christian hard rock, and as mentioned above, this was even part of his reason for coming to Livets Ord. The criticism of rock music was a very important factor in his leaving the congregation in the winter of 1992/93.[13] As I do in this chapter, he of course also viewed this criticism as a major change in policy, one that also resulted in a major change in his own life.

To my direct questions, Håkan had no definite answer as to what had brought on this change in policy, but he believed that one important reason was related to criticism of the lifestyle of Christian musicians. Two examples of this emerged from my discussion with Håkan, regarding hair length and smoking.

The first example deals with hair. As is well known, male heavy metal musicians commonly wear their hair long, and this is often also the case within Christian metal. Long hair on men is (or at least was at this time) not acceptable within Livets Ord. Håkan says that Jerusalem's vocalist Ulf Christiansson cut his hair when entering Bible school, and also talks of a musician from another Swedish Christian metal band that he recalls as causing a bit of a problem to the school because he initially refused to cut his hair. Håkan also recalls another young man (apparently not a musician), who was expelled from the school because his hair was too long.

Håkan also recalls one particular story given as explanation of the change in policy on rock music. As he remembers it, Ulf Ekman stated in a sermon that he had come to hear about about some shady activities among the members of the group Petra. Ekman did not specify, but Håkan tells of the following rumour that circulated in the congregation:

> According to this story, a Livets Ord member was working at the check in counter at Arlanda airport when Petra had had a gig . . . in Stockholm. And when they left and were checking in, this person from Livets Ord was checking them in and asked if they wanted smoking or non smoking and they chose smoking.

He specifies that he was told this story by a girl who wanted to use it as a strong warning against the music he was still listening too. Håkan also feels that most members would not have found the smoking a great sin, and thinks that it was clever of Ekman to be so unspecific and leave the details up the imagination of the members of the congregation. As these examples show, lifestyle issues were important in the approach to rock music in Livets Ord at this time. The focus on lifestyle is also clear in many cases of Livets Ord's criticism of rock music (see e.g. Arnroth 1993). Ekman (1993a) also emphasises this theme. He speaks of a visit to Gothenburg, where by chance he stayed at the same hotel as some Christian musicians playing at an annual Christian rock festival at the Scandinavium arena in the same city:

> They were shocked when they saw me. We met there at that hotel, there is a large entrance area and there is a pub there or a bar, and there they sat, the whole gang. I won't tell you what they held in their hands, but one could say that it wasn't Bibles or hymnals so to speak. They have no right to come and spew[14] forth their music with their miserable lifestyle.

It is clear from the quote that the musicians in the pub had some previous relation to Ekman. He assumes that they recognised him and had reason to believe that he recognised them, and that he would not approve of their choice of activity – 'they were shocked when they saw me'. The fact that Ekman does not want to name the objects the musicians held in their hands – perhaps beer glasses, if they were in a pub – can be taken as an indication that these things are considered so impure that they should not even be mentioned by a Christian, or at least not by a pastor in a sermon. The last sentence of the quote explicitly states that this lifestyle – sitting in a pub without Bibles and hymnals – denies the musicians their right to communicate their music.

Other possible explanations for the change in policy on rock music, beside lifestyle issues, were also mentioned by Håkan. He says that there were other similar sudden changes during his time at Livets Ord, e.g. in the attitude towards European integration. This could be seen as a way of testing the members' loyalty, or as Håkan says:

> They perhaps didn't want people to leave the congregation, but they wanted to purge it, so to speak, of people with too strong a will of their own . . . it didn't matter much if a question like this crossed over the line so that some people

left because this showed that they had trouble subordinating themselves.

Ekman's views on leadership issues and in particular on the relations between pastor, musicians and congregation apparently played a part in the change of policy on Christian rock music. It is quite clear that Livets Ord is an organisation very much centred on Ulf Ekman. Ekman can be seen as a charismatic leader typical of a sect-type organisation, and his position as leader is clearly an important factor in the criticism of Christian rock.

Criticism of rock and the group Jerusalem

None of the documented Livets Ord critique of Christian hard rock that I have come across explicitly mentions Jerusalem. The musicians at the hotel pub in Gothenburg may or may not have been members of Jerusalem, but the fact that the reported incident occurred in the group's home town, and that Jerusalem has played at the Scandinavium festival several times (Jerusalem 2000; jerusalem.ovanmolnen.com) should be enough to at least give the listeners cause to suspect that the group may be indicated.[15]

A more direct allusion to Jerusalem and Ulf Christiansson is the ironic comment Ekman (1993a) makes about the above-mentioned expectations of a music from heaven:

> Some think that heavenly music is some complicated melodies that will come sometime at the end of the nineties, that some new music will come from heaven . . . They do nothing before, like, the end of the nineties, they sit and wait for it to come. Stop doing that!

Since Christiansson was the person linked to these expectations of a 'heavenly music', it seems evident that he would be the person most clearly indicated in this quote.

It is also evident that the members of Jerusalem somehow felt that their possibilities of remaining in Livets Ord were running out during this time, and they left the congregation and moved back to Gothenburg. Jerusalem did not leave organised Christianity when they left Livets Ord, or even the faith movement. They (or at least

Christiansson) actually joined the same congregation in Gothenburg that Ekman had visited when he saw the musicians at the hotel pub (Ekman 1993a; *Trons Värld* 1993b: 18).

As mentioned above, in 1993 both *Magazinet* and *Trons Värld* ran articles strongly critical of Christian rock, and particularly hard rock, albeit without mentioning Jerusalem. There were also at least a few articles in *Trons Värld* with a different tendency, e.g. an interview with Ulf Christiansson (conducted not by the magazine's music critic but by the chief editor) in connection with the move from Uppsala and the comeback of Jerusalem, and a review of a concert with the group then briefly called 'New Jerusalem'.

In the interview (*Trons Värld* 1993b: 18–19) Christiansson says that he is grateful for the time at Livets Ord, and that it has given him 'a new vision and the power to realise it'. The content of this vision is revealed in his statement that: 'At the end of last year God started talking to me and my family about moving back to Gothenburg and starting Jerusalem again.'

It is noteworthy that the time period mentioned in this quote: 'the end of last year', i.e. the end of 1992, coincided with the period when a strong criticism of Christian rock becomes apparent at Livets Ord. There is also an interesting similarity between this quote and one of the above quotes from Ekman, where he says that the holy spirit talked to him about Christian rock. God talks to both Ekman and Christiansson, but with very different messages: instead of declaring that Christian rock will be eaten by dogs (which is the metaphor Ekman uses), God has talked to Christiansson about launching the pioneer Scandinavian Christian rock group Jerusalem again. Both Ekman and Christiansson use the – to them absolutely realistic – claim that God has spoken to them as a means of legitimating their respective views on the topic.

Christiansson also comments on the 'music from heaven' theme in the same interview and says that waiting for 'something complicated, almost mystical' can bring you 'to a dead end'. He seems to agree with Ekman's assessment of the wait for a music from heaven, but the solution is different:

> This thing about music and musical styles is really very simple. We must understand what the language of the people

of today is. What is it that a whole world listens to? There is no doubt that the answer is that all the youth of the world listen to rock music, rap, soul, etc. (*Trons Värld* 1993b: 18–19)

It is clear that the emphasis on separation from the world, which had previously been very strong, has now given way to an ambition to be a part of contemporary culture. The conclusion of the article takes up the same theme: 'God has given [Christiansson] a language and a style that makes young people understand and listen.'

The concert review (*Trons Värld* 1993b: 19) of the first concert under the name 'New Jerusalem' seems to agree. The review begins:

'Finally', many in the audience exclaimed when Ulf Christiansson, 'Uffe', struck the first heavy chords. Because very many of them have missed this band, who with their clear preaching of Christ since the end of the 70s were pioneers of Christian rock music.

The interview and the review take a completely different stand both towards Jerusalem and Christian rock in general than do Ekman's (1993a) sermons, previous articles in the same magazine (e.g. *Trons Värld* 1993a: 16) and the special issue on Christian rock of *Magazinet* (1993a) to follow a few months later. This indicates that Livets Ord's change in policy on Christian rock music was not clear-cut by any means, and that an influential person such as the owner and chief editor of *Trons Värld* could express a different opinion and still remain a member of the congregation (which he did for a few more years, as he told me in my interview with him).

In the first quote in the introduction to this chapter, the band-history info on the Jerusalem website describes the Livets Ord experience in positive terms: 'Jesus was put first.' The departure is accounted for in the website band-history in the following way:

But the vision and the dream [to make records] was still alive. In 1992, the band moved back to Gothenburg and made the album 'Prophet'. It became the album to get the most favourable reviews. (*Jerusalem*)

There is no tendency to describe any kind of conflict situation. Both events, becoming members of Livets Ord and leaving the congregation, are described in less than dramatic terms, as geographical moves, and as parts of a logical – almost natural, as it were – continuum.

In an article for the Swedish Christian music magazine *Noizegate Music* (2005: 6–11), several of the members of the group describe the period in Livets Ord and their leaving the congregation in similar terms, focusing on geography. Keyboard player Reidar Paulsen refers to the period by mentioning the band's own studio and the fact that 'at that time it was in Uppsala'. The strongest statement comes from bass player Peter Carlsohn, who says 'we were up in Uppsala and there was some turbulence too, regarding music and all that'. There is no mention of the reason they were in Uppsala, and only the word 'turbulence' gives an indication of why they left.

The band-history on the website gives 1992 as the year of Jerusalem's move to Gothenburg. The *Trons Värld* interview published in August 1993, which refers to a (reviewed) concert that had been held 'at the end of July', is said to have been conducted 'on the veranda of Ulf Christiansson's house in Storvreta outside Uppsala' (*Trons Värld* 1993b: 18–19). Christiansson also says that the band, crew and family members, approximately 40 people, were moving to Gothenburg 'in the beginning of September' 1993. As quoted above, he also said that 'God started talking' to him about moving at the end of 1992. I see this as an interesting example of how different representations of an event, even when produced by the same person or group of people, may differ even as to such 'hard' facts as dating the represented event. A possible interpretation is that the Jerusalem members actually left the congregation in 1992, but did not move to Gothenburg immediately, and later described the departure from the congregation as a geographical move to de-emphasise a conflict between the band members and Livets Ord.

In the Questions & Answers section of the website,[16] a fan points out that the songs from the album *Dancing on the Head of the Serpent*, recorded during the Livets Ord period, no longer feature at the concerts, and wants to know why: 'Is it because of bad memories from Livets Ord, or what?' Christiansson answers that he thinks the record is good, that they have no special feelings about it either way, but that they have more than 300 songs and have elected to play the older songs, as well as songs from *Prophet*. He says that the fans like the older songs, and gives no other explanation of why they have made this choice.[17]

Another fan in the same forum on the band's website gives his view of Jerusalem's career and states that 'not much of value to us fans' occurred during the Livets Ord period. Christiansson responds – several years after the departure from Livets Ord[18] – and says that the time the group spent in the congregation was

> of good use to the whole band . . . Even if there were some conflicts at the end of that time, it still was a time of rest and re-evaluation that we without doubt needed, but it perhaps took too much time, hard to know.

Here Christiansson on the one hand admits that there were conflicts at the end of the period, but he still wants to defend the band's decision to join Livets Ord, and as I see it also the congregation itself. He does not specify what the conflicts were, and with whom, but since their departure occured during the time of heightened criticism of Christian rock music, I draw the conclusion that there was a connection between the two.

Håkan draws the same conclusion. He even suggests that the conflicts are documented on the Jerusalem album *Prophet* from 1994 – 'probably one of the best records they've ever made' [sic] according to the band's website.[19] A track titled 'Truth' talks of false prophets:

> If he covers truth with a cheap excuse
> In the end he'll lose 'cause he left the truth
> [. . .]
> Prophets that are false will not pay the cost
> Do not really care what is true or not
> You will be confused when they speak to you[20]

Håkan interprets this as a description of Ulf Ekman:

> On the record *Prophet* there are very clear allusions to Ulf Ekman . . . I bought that record and thought woah[21] now Ulf Christiansson has refused to answer journalists' questions . . . he hasn't wanted to comment on his relationship to Livets Ord, but there he distances himself from it, and talks of prophets who allege that they speak for God . . .

Of course it sounds possible that an artist would express his or her point of view in artistic work rather than in interviews, but to a person (such as myself) with limited first-hand experience of the context, the allusions to particular contemporary persons in the lyrics of the Jerusalem song 'Truth' are not at all clear. I therefore find it all the more interesting and enlightening to have been made aware of Håkan's interpretation of the lyrics, as one of many different repre-sentations of the encounter between the rock group Jerusalem and the Livets Ord congregation.

Concluding remarks

This chapter has considered the time spent by the Christian hard rock group Jerusalem in the neo-Pentecostal Livets Ord congregation in Uppsala, Sweden.

This sojourn may be of some interest in itself. But above all I find it interesting as an example of the relationship of Christianity to a popular cultural phenomenon such as popular music, and to contemporary society in general. It is also a case of the specific relationship of a sect type of religious organisation to the surrounding society, and the study provides some concrete examples of the form such a relationship can take.

The case shows that the relationship between institutionalised religion, specifically a sect-type organisation, and contemporary society and culture, can be quite complicated in several ways. Firstly, it is hardly possible to draw an absolute line of defence against contempo-rary society, or even against such a limited phenomenon as rock music. When the criticism was strong against secular rock, Christian rock was endorsed and played in the church; and even when the criticism against Christian rock was very harsh at Livets Ord, contemporary musical instruments such as drums and electric guitars were used in the services. Secondly, it is clear that the lines are contested in several ways. Differing opinions are voiced not only privately but also in print, as in the articles on Jerusalem in *Trons Värld* (1993b), and members of the congregation express their dissent by leaving – as did Håkan, interviewed for this chapter, as well as the members of Jerusalem.

Thirdly, the examples studied show that boundary lines may change over time, as the main point of interest in the empirical material

presented here is the apparently quite sudden change in policy at Livets
Ord, from endorsing to strongly criticising Christian rock. In addition
to the examples discussed above, it must be noted that the position on
Christian rock has changed again at Livets Ord.[22] Since the end of the
1990s rock concerts have been held again at the congregation – I have
personally attended several – and Christian rock music is sold in the
shop at the church, and in the web shop on the congregation's website
livetsord.se – including several albums by Jerusalem as well as by Ulf
Christiansson.

The legitimation of a sect-type religious organisation such as Livets
Ord is to a large extent based on the maintenance of sharp dichotomies. It is essential for the existence of the organisation to maintain
clear boundaries between the values, expressions and people that are
included and those that are excluded. From a sociological point of
view, it is clear that such boundaries are never set in stone, but always
constructed, and never absolute, but always negotiated. It has been the
aim of this chapter to provide some concrete examples of the complexity of such negotiations.

2

Christian Metal in Finland

Institutional religion and popular music in the midst of religious change

Marcus Moberg

Introduction

Metal has been a highly polarising and controversial form of music ever since its emergence in the late 1960s and early 1970s. However, in addition to being one of the most debated forms of popular music of our time, it has also proved to be one of the most enduringly appealing and long-lived. Stark and austere themes from the world of religion and myth have always constituted one of metal's most important sources of lyrical and aesthetic inspiration. Today a wide range of alternative religious/spiritual themes and ideas are disseminated through an increasingly globalised metal culture. At the same time, much of metal culture is also marked by an antagonism towards certain forms of religion, and institutional Christianity in particular (Partridge 2005: 246–55; Moberg 2009a: 121–2; Moberg 2009b: 137–41). It is not surprising, then, that no other form of contemporary popular music has been as consistently condemned by conservative Christian groups as metal.

In light of this, Christian metal music, which emerged in the USA in the early 1980s, can be viewed as a paradoxical or at the very least peculiar phenomenon. Even so, recent years have seen the development of a highly independent transnational Christian metal scene.[1]

This constitutes an exceptionally good example of a space in which Christianity and a particular popular music culture have met and merged. It can be understood as a cross-denominational alternative Christian space in which people from a number of countries, with a wide range of different denominational backgrounds and affiliations, and a passion for metal music, can meet. This space is not directly sponsored or controlled by any particular Christian institution and it advocates no particular denominational teachings or creed.

When talking about Christian metal it is important to note that it has embraced metal's defining musical, aesthetic and stylistic elements wholeheartedly. Although Christian metal constitutes a largely separate and independent metal scene, it should by no means be regarded as a separate metal style or sub-genre and must be seen against the musical and aesthetic backdrop of metal music and culture in general. The differences between Christian and 'secular' metal are to be found in their respective discourses. The similarities outweigh the differences by far. The main purpose of Christian metal has always been to express and spread the Christian faith through the metal styles that already exist. However, these days Christian metal musicians would not necessarily accept such a narrow description of their musical endeavours. This is because, for many, Christian metal is about much more than merely the 'appropriation' or 'borrowing' of the music and style of metal for purely religious or evangelistic purposes. Many Christian metal musicians and fans see themselves as ordinary 'metalheads' who choose to express their faith through their music. For many Christian metal musicians and fans today, Christian metal is viewed as an alternative and fully legitimate Christian lifestyle (Moberg 2009a: 134–5).

So how should the phenomenon of Christian metal be understood in relation to broader contemporary changes and transformations of religious life and practice throughout much of the Western world? In this regard Finland provides a particularly interesting case for two particular reasons. First, Finland is among very few countries (perhaps the only one) in the world where metal enjoys the status of mainstream music in the fullest sense of the word. Second, although Christian popular music reached Finland long ago, the Christian metal scene is so far the only distinct Christian popular music culture to have developed on a large scale. Indeed, contemporary Finland is probably the best place to start when examining the relationship between religion and popular music more generally (Moberg 2009a: 2). And although secularisation has not been as thoroughgoing in Finland as in many other Western European countries, Finnish society and culture have clearly not remained untouched by broader contemporary transformations of religious life and practice.

The purpose of this chapter is twofold: first, to provide a short general overview of the contemporary transnational and Finnish Christian metal scene; and second, to situate the Finnish Christian metal scene within the particular religious and cultural context of Finland and offer some observations on what it might imply about broader processes of religious change in this particular context. The largely electronic media-based global popular cultural milieu has increasingly come to transcend particular social and cultural contexts (Clark 2006: 475; Lynch 2005: 56–7). This means that it is also necessary to look at how the Finnish Christian metal scene is affected by being part of a wider transnational phenomenon.

Christian metal: Historical development and contemporary scenes

Christian metal, or 'white metal' as it was also called during its earlier phase, took off at the beginning of the 1980s when bands such as Saint, Messiah Prophet and Stryper from the USA, as well as Leviticus from Sweden, appeared with a full-blown metal sound and look and the express purpose of spreading the Christian message to secular metal audiences. Much like its secular counterpart, however, it quickly became a highly controversial form of Christian rock (Brown 2005: 118). Christian metal diversified considerably in the late 1980s and early 1990s, essentially following in the footsteps of the overall development of secular metal. These days, Christian metal comprises all metal subgenres and styles, including extreme styles such as thrash, death and black metal (also called 'unblack') (Thompson 2000, 163–4; Moberg 2009a: 128). We should also note here that Nordic bands have played a prominent role in the development of Christian metal since the mid-1990s.

Christian metal did not gain a strong foothold outside North America until the late 1980s and early 1990s. Today, particularly significant and active scenes can be found in the Nordic countries Sweden, Norway and Finland. Christian metal has also spread to other north-western European countries such as Germany, the Netherlands and Belgium and to a lesser extent Denmark and the UK. In addition, larger Christian metal scenes have also developed in some Latin American countries with growing and significant Protestant minorities such as Brazil and Mexico. However as Christian metal is firmly rooted in evangelical Protestantism (broadly defined), on the whole it has so far remained more rare, though not entirely nonexistent, in most predominantly Catholic countries (Moberg 2009a: 172).

Today's transnational scene has developed its own highly independent and largely Internet-based infrastructure of record labels, promotion and distribution channels, magazines, fanzines, webzines, online communities and festivals (Moberg 2008: 91–2; 2009a: 180–203). In recent years, the small Christian metal scenes of Europe have played an increasingly significant role in these developments. There is also a great deal of cooperation between people involved in maintaining this infrastructure throughout the core regions of the transnational scene. In this way, the scene as a whole has developed into a transnational cross-denominational community characterised by a set of shared aims and concerns.

Defining Christian metal

As Christian metal has developed and diversified, so have various understandings of its definition, main purposes and aims. First of all, Christian metal is typically defined as metal that somehow conveys a Christian *message*. This means that in order to be considered truly Christian, bands are required to convey a Christian content through their lyrics in some form or other. However, there is no agreement within the scene as to what exactly counts as 'Christian content'. Indeed, in this context, a Christian lyrical content is usually defined very broadly, for example as reflecting Christian values, as conveying a Christian message, as approaching things from a Christian perspective, or as reflecting a Christian world view. Christian metal is also commonly defined as metal that is made and produced *by* people who are themselves professed Christians. Sometimes, Christian metal is defined as being principally produced *for* Christian audiences as well. Lastly, Christian metal is sometimes defined as metal that is produced and distributed through various Christian networks guided by an evangelistic agenda. Such notions usually stem from ideas regarding the 'gatekeeping' functions of Christian labels, producers and distributors which are seen as being in a position to be able to guarantee to some extent that the albums they release, produce or distribute are made by Christians and contain some form of Christian content. These days, however, releasing records on secular labels has become increasingly acceptable, if not actually desirable, as long as bands which do so still conform to the other two 'requirements' outlined above.[2]

These issues are constantly being debated within the wider contemporary transnational scene. It is important, though, to note that debates such as these constitute important components of the internal discourse of just about any music scene. In this case, however, they are also highly symptomatic of the ongoing processes of negotiation concerned with legitimating and securing a place for Christian metal within a broader, and sometimes hostile, popular cultural context without making too many compromises regarding its Christian distinctiveness along the way (Moberg 2009a: 145–6).

As I have argued elsewhere, a number of key discourses on the basic meaning and function of Christian metal are also circulating within today's transnational scene (Moberg 2009a: 204–29). These discourses represent Christian metal as an alternative form of religious expression, as an alternative, and often effective, means of evangelism, as a fully legitimate form of religious expression and evangelism, and as a positive alternative to secular metal. Approaching Christian metal by focusing on its discursive construction essentially means approaching it from the perspective of Christian metal musicians and fans themselves. The point to note is that the scene as a whole is discursively constructed in terms of an open cross-denominational community or movement with a shared set of aims and goals. At the same time, it is also important to note that, for Christian metalheads themselves, participating in Christian metal scenes is also very much about meeting like-minded people and having fun (Moberg 2009a: 276).

Christian metal in Finland

Bands playing heavier forms of Christian rock did not appear in Finland until the late 1980s. The Christian hard rock band Terapia, formed in 1987, is commonly regarded as having been particularly influential for the subsequent development of Finnish Christian metal. Another influential Christian hard rock band, The Rain, also formed in 1987, has remained widely popular among Christian audiences to this day. In the beginning of the 1990s, a few Christian metal bands proper, playing extreme metal styles, started to appear. The Christian extreme metal band DBM (Destroyer of Black Metal), formed in 1990, and is usually regarded as the first Finnish Christian metal band. Having released a few demos, the band split after a few years. Former members of DBM, Manu Lehtinen and Aki Särkioja, later went on to form two of Finland's most influential Christian metal bands, both of which have enjoyed considerable international success. In 1991, Särkioja formed the Christian death metal band Immortal Souls. Manu Lehtinen went on to form another influential Christian death metal group, Deuteronomium, in 1993.[3] Both are still active today.

By the mid-1990s a small and tightly-knit scene had emerged, and by the end of the decade a few national media channels, labels and annual festivals had been established as well. In 1998, Deuteronomium band members Manu Lehtinen and Miika Partala established the company Little Rose Productions which functioned simultaneously as a Christian metal importer, distributor and record label. It was the first of its kind in Finland. The record distribution/retail wing of Little Rose Productions was eventually sold to Lasse Niskala and Päivi Niemi, who established Maanalainen Levykauppa (The Underground Record Store) which has become one of the largest Christian music retailers in the country. In recent years, it has also expanded its activities and started releasing records by Finnish bands. The end of the 1990s also saw the establishment of two Finnish-language Christian metal fanzines, *The Christian Underground Zine* (now defunct) and *Ristillinen Metal Magazine*.[4] The latter has remained active to this day with seven published issues at the time of writing. The Finnish scene has also created its own Finnish-language Christian metal online discussion forum called Kristillinen metalliunioni (Christian Metal Union).[5]

Finland also has an unusually large number of annual festivals featuring Christian metal bands. Among these, the Immortal Metal Fest, established in 2001, is dedicated exclusively to Christian metal. It is held each spring in the small town of Nokia. The festival has grown significantly in recent years and is now one of the most important annual Christian metal festivals in the Nordic countries. It currently attracts around 500 participants each year, mainly from Finland, and has featured many well-known bands from all over the world. It has evolved into one of the Finnish scene's most important institutions. In addition, the annual three-day Christian youth festival Maata näkyvissä (Land in sight) – the largest of its kind in the Nordic countries – always features the immensely popular so-called 'Alternatiivi pommisuoja' ('The alternative bunker') Christian metal concert. This particular concert, which usually features short sets by three or four bands, has developed into an important national showcase for Finnish Christian metal bands. The concert is held in a space that accommodates up to 1,000 people and is nearly always sold out. This particular event affords Christian bands exposure to a wider, and predominantly young, Christian audience. In addition, in 2005 a midsummer festival called OHM-Fest (Organised Hard Music Group festival) featuring Christian metal bands was established in the town of Keuruu. In 2008, it was organised by Maanalainen Levykauppa under the name of Maanalainen juhannus (Underground midsummer). A smaller annual event called True Attitude has also been held in the town of Heinola since 2005. A few one-off festivals have also been organised in recent years. Lastly, many Christian metal bands have also played the Christian rock festival Ristirock (Cross Rock) held in the city of Tampere each year (Moberg 2009a: 177).

In addition to these larger events, separate concerts are also held regularly in venues throughout the country, especially in the Helsinki metropolitan area. Such concerts and events are usually held in the youth cafés of particular denominations, usually the Evangelical Lutheran Church. For example, the church's Hard Gospel Café in Helsinki has regularly organised 'Gospel Nights' featuring Christian metal bands since 2000. Compared to many other countries, the Finnish scene has established an unusually large number of its own events. In addition to these, some bands also play secular venues (Moberg 2009a: 177–8).

The Finnish scene has grown steadily since the end of the 1990s. At present it contains around 20 active bands, many of which have become successful within the wider international scene. New bands are also constantly being formed while others disband. Some bands may only be active for a shorter period while others continue to play for many years. However, as with any music scene, the number of people actively involved is difficult to assess. As mentioned, the annual Immortal Metal Fest attracts around 500 participants each year. This number corresponds roughly the number of people actively involved in the scene as a whole. However, when people who only engage with the scene sporadically are included, one could presume that the number rises to around 1,000. This, however, is a tentative estimate. It is important to note that not all members of the scene participate in the same ways or to the same extent. We might define an 'actively involved' scene member as one who regularly buys new Christian metal records, follows various forms of specialised Christian metal media, participates in discourse on the subject (for example in online discussion forums) and regularly attends concerts and events. Most active scene members are young adult males. Female scene members have, however, become an increasingly visible group within the scene. Most belong to the religiously active minority of the Evangelical Lutheran Church, but many are also members of free churches (e.g. Charismatic or Pentecostal). The majority are also overt metalheads (Moberg 2009a: 178–9).

The Christian metal scene has become particularly concentrated in certain regional areas. This is simply to say that more bands tend to come from these areas, and that events are more frequently organised there. Among these, the Helsinki metropolitan area and surrounding towns is the most vibrant. This is not surprising considering the capital's near-total position of dominance as the cultural and economic centre of the country. The scene is also relatively active in areas around the city of Tampere in the southwest of the country, around the city of Jyväskylä in the centre of the country, and throughout the region of Ostrobotnia on the northwest coast. However, the scene has not become divided into different local scenes. Because of its small scale, it has remained very much national in scale. For example, larger events attract fans from all over the country. The Finnish scene could well be described as close-knit. People actively involved in Christian metal tend to know each other well and also to be very knowledgeable about the scene as a whole. The large number of festivals and events also provides them with regular opportunities to meet. In this way, the scene has also become a recognisable space within wider Finnish Christian circles. As mentioned above, many events are directly church-sponsored. However, it is important to note that, as with the wider international scene, the Finnish scene is expressly constructed as a space where denominational affiliation is of no real importance (Moberg 2009a: 179–80).

Christian metal has also become more visible within wider Finnish culture in recent years. This is largely due to the establishment of a special 'metal service' called the Metal Mass which has been organised by the Evangelical Lutheran Church since the summer of 2006. These are traditional Lutheran services (the term 'mass' refers to the Eucharist being included) held in full accordance with traditional Lutheran liturgy. The difference is that all featured music, of both liturgy and collectively sung hymns, is accompanied by a metal band. The Metal Mass has managed to attract much larger crowds than conventional church services and has gradually evolved into an institution in itself. However, on its official web page, the creators of the Metal Mass are careful to point out that it is a church service and not a concert.[6] The metal bands featured at these services largely comprise Finnish Christian metal musicians. In a sense, the Metal Mass has developed into an institution of the Finnish Christian metal scene as well. For one thing, its success has clearly afforded the scene some increased wider visibility (Moberg 2009a: 196).

Popular culture and religious change

Recent decades have seen significant changes in the religious landscape throughout much of the West. Christopher Partridge has argued that contemporary Western society and culture is experiencing a process of 're-enchantment' (Partridge 2004, 2005). Similarly, Paul Heelas and Linda Woodhead have pointed to how the overall 'massive subjective turn' of Western culture and society may have sparked the beginning of a 'spiritual revolution' (Heelas and Woodhead 2005). However, as these scholars point out, the contemporary religious landscape of the

West may still need to be understood within an overarching framework of secularisation: a situation that has long been interpreted as posing great challenges to traditional and institutional Christianity, for which the overall picture has long been one of slow but steady decline (see for example Martin 2005: 8).

An important part of the secularisation debate concerns the emergence of alternative forms of religion and spirituality in the West. Scholars concentrating on these developments often point out the ways in which the contemporary religious landscape is simultaneously marked by processes of secularisation as well as of sacralisation/re-sacralisation (for example Partridge 2004; Heelas and Woodhead 2005). The overall effects of secularisation on institutional religion are in no way refuted by these scholars. They do, however, question the validity of claims that secularisation somehow automatically and irreversibly has led, and will continue to lead, to an overall decline in religious vitality and individual religiosity as such. Instead, it is argued that religious belief and practice has changed and been transformed in contemporary society and culture, appearing in new forms, new ways, and new places (Moberg 2009a: 60).

According to Partridge, these significant changes in the spiritual landscape of the West have important implications for the study of religion itself: 'Just as we are witnessing a revolution in the way twenty-first century religion/spirituality is lived, so there will need to be a revolution in the way it is studied and understood' (Partridge 2004: 59). Importantly, it is argued that particular attention should be directed at the role of *popular culture* in this process (Partridge 2004: 84–5). This is evident in the ways in which popular culture has become an increasingly important and natural source of inspiration for many people's construction of religious and spiritual identities regardless of their particular religious affiliations (Partridge 2004: 121; see also Hoover 2006; Heelas and Seel 2003: 236). As argued by Stewart M. Hoover, these developments have also made it increasingly important to account for the ways in which people's actual religious and spiritual beliefs are reflected in various forms of media and popular culture as they are used by specific religious or spiritual groups and, moreover, to explore the different ways and degrees to which particular media and popular cultural forms may indeed become *formative* and *determinative* of such groups.[7] One should also keep in mind that today's wider popular cultural milieu in itself has come to constitute an ever more important arena where that which 'counts' as 'religion' is constantly contested and negotiated (Mahan 2007: 51; Chidester 2005, 9; Schultze 2001: 46).

The current state of religion in Finland

The Finnish religious landscape has been dominated by the Evangelical Lutheran Church ever since the Protestant Reformation reached the Kingdom of Sweden at the end of the sixteenth century. As of 31 December 2008, 80.7 per cent of all Finns were members of the Evangelical Lutheran Church.[8] There is evidence of a steady rise of interest in alternative religious/spiritual teachings, but membership of alternative religious/spiritual groups has so far remained low (Sohlberg 2008: 211–15). The dominant social position of the Evangelical Lutheran Church, its special legal relationship to the state, as well as its position as *the* Church in public discourse, means that people affiliated with other Christian churches, and indeed other religions, cannot altogether ignore the dealings of the Evangelical Lutheran Church (Moberg 2009a: 69–70).

The current state of religion in Finland has received a great deal of attention from Finnish scholars of religion in recent years. In their overview of current trends in Finnish religiosity, *Religion in Finland. Decline, Change and Transformation of Finnish Religiosity*, Kimmo Kääriäinen, Kati Niemelä and Kimmo Ketola (2005) approach the issue of whether Finland has 'gone secular' in the light of the traditional and most commonly used ways of quantitatively measuring religiosity in connection to theories of secularisation and religious change. They offer the following general observations about the state of religion in contemporary Finland. The dominant Evangelical Lutheran Church has seen a steady, but by no means radical, decline in membership (about 10 per cent) during the past five decades. The significance attached to the doctrines and religious message of the Church has also declined. Participation in all forms of Church activities, particularly activities that require long-term commitment, has also declined sharply, especially among younger age groups. However, according to Kääriäinen, Niemelä and Ketola, Church members' attitudes to their own membership as such has largely remained unchanged; that is, the majority of Church members still view membership of the Church as something natural and taken for granted (Kääriäinen, Niemelä and Ketola 2005: 166–8; cf. Moberg 2009a: 71–2). In relation to British sociologist of religion Grace Davie's oft-cited description of Britons as 'believing without belonging' (Davie 1994), Finns have instead been described as 'belonging without believing' (Martin 2005: 86) or, indeed, as 'believing in belonging' (Kääriäinen, Niemelä and Ketola 2005: 85).

Above all, Finnish religiosity has become increasingly *privatised*. Although participation in all forms of Church activity has seen an overall decline, there seem to have only been slight changes in the degree of private religious practice. For example, the percentage of people believing in the existence of God has not changed significantly since the mid-1970s, and the share of people who pray on a regular basis has also remained relatively stable. Thus, compared to the rest of Europe, Finnish private religious practice appears to have remained relatively high (Kääriäinen, Niemelä and Ketola 2005: 170; cf. Moberg 2009a: 72).

Studying young adults' religious sensibilities is particularly important in this context because it provides valuable insights into possible future developments in the religious attitudes of Finns (Mikkola et al. 2007). The religiosity of young Finnish adults appears to have declined on all fronts. Viewed as a group, young adults today are generally less interested in religion than they were a few decades ago. This, of course, also has to do with a more widespread weakening of religious socialisation, particularly as received in the home (Niemelä and Koivula 2006: 176). Young people are also more inclined to emphasise individual and subjective values. Indeed, Mikkola, Niemelä and Petterson highlight the important role played by the media in the formation of young adults' views on religion and the increasingly important role being played by popular culture as a source of religious/spiritual inspiration (Mikkola et al. 2007: 44–9, 82, 101; cf. Moberg 2009a: 72–3).

But what about the *religiously active* minority within the Church? Generally speaking, religiously active young members of the Church have become increasingly frustrated by entrenched and drawn-out debates within the Church on topics such as resistance to female clergy and homosexuality. As Mikkola, Niemelä and Petterson put it, 'in the opinion of the religiously active minority, the Church is not sufficiently bold in taking a stand' (Mikkola, Niemelä and Petterson 2007: 69). Indeed, the Church's ambivalent stance on many doctrinal and moral issues may indeed 'activate those active in the Church to drift away from it' (ibid.). However, as the authors go on to point out, the 'religiously active' do not constitute a homogeneous group. Some identify with the 'Church mainstream' and tend to regard religion as a mainly private matter. Others, however, identify more with revivalist views. It is from within this group in particular that the Church is often criticised for 'its lack of backbone and for not being faithful enough to the Bible' (ibid: 76). People within this group tend to participate less in ordinary Church activity, favouring instead a deeper engagement with different forms of revivalist activities practised by particular groups within the Church or some other Christian denomination. As Helen Cameron points out, modern churches of today often include 'affinity groups within particular denominations and cross-denominational groups meeting to explore particular spiritualities' (Cameron 2003: 117). She goes on to argue that, as 'These groups build trust on the basis of shared experience . . . It seems possible that affiliation to these groups may strengthen at the expense of participation in the local church' (Ibid.). Research on the religiosity of young adults in Finland also indicates clearly that the *experiential* aspects of religious activity have become increasingly important over time (Niemelä 2006: 65; Mikkola, Niemelä and Petterson 2007: 75–6, 127). Although there are a number of such groups within the broader Christian environment of Finland today, the Christian metal scene could also be seen as an example of such a cross-denominational affinity group based on shared experience (cf. Moberg 2009a: 73).

The Church has also introduced a number of strategies and nationwide projects aimed at bringing young people back into the fold. The general idea of such projects has been to try to approach young people on their own terms. Attention has also been directed at the issue of music in Church settings. It is recognised that traditional church music no longer appeals to younger age groups. So the Church has experimented with alternative forms of music. The Metal Mass mentioned above is one of the clearest examples of this. Then there is also the issue of language (Mikkola et al. 2007: 128–36; cf. Moberg 2009a: 74).

These observations all concern the members of the Finnish Christian metal scene, many of whom belong to the religiously active minority of the Evangelical Lutheran Church, and all of whom belong to the broader 'active Christian minority' of the country.

The contemporary Finnish religious climate is marked by some contradictory trends. Although the general trend has been one of slow decline of organised religion, the vast majority of all Finns have nevertheless remained members of the dominant Evangelical Lutheran Church. However, religious belief and practice has become increasingly privatised, with fewer and fewer people, particularly young adults, feeling that institutional religion has much to offer them. Increasing numbers of young people in particular no longer seem to feel a need to belong to the church (Mikkola, Niemelä and Petterson 2007: 68; cf. Moberg 2009a: 75). In other words, people seem to have become increasingly estranged from Church doctrine, while the appreciation of the Church as a social institution has remained high (Miikola, Niemelä and Petterson 2007: 80–83, 94–95). On account of these contradictory factors, the time does not yet seem ripe for more confident predictions about the future of Finnish religiosity.

The Finnish Christian metal scene in context

How, then, should the Finnish Christian metal scene be understood when situated within the broader Finnish cultural and religious context of today? In my own research on the Finnish scene, I have focused on the ways in which it functions and figures within the everyday religious lives of its core members and musicians in particular (Moberg 2009). Regardless of their denominational affiliations, Finnish Christian metal musicians tend to emphasise a need for new, alternative and complementary forms of religious expression among younger generations across the denominational spectrum. And considering the weakening role and position of Christian churches throughout Finnish society at large, scene members also tend to point out that more traditional ways of attracting people to churches clearly have not been able to meet the challenges of today. In this way, musicians also invest their own activities as well as the scene as a whole with an evangelistic mandate. However, as the Christian metal scene does not attach any particular importance to denominational affiliation, there is really no reason why scene members should aim to attract people to particular churches. This is why the Christian metal scene should not be equated directly with the practices or aims of particular churches. For, although the members of the Finnish Christian metal scene represent many different denominations and remain active within their respective parishes, they also participate actively in the maintenance and reproduction of a distinct Christian music scene in which denominational affiliation plays no real role. As mentioned above, in transnational discourse on the subject, Christian metal is typically represented as constituting an alternative form of religious expression, an alternative means of evangelism, a fully legitimate form of religious expression and evangelism, and an alternative to secular metal. Finnish scene members are also clearly influenced by these key ways of representing Christian metal. In particular, musicians tend to represent their own musical activities as constituting an alternative form of religious expression and evangelism. They also tend to express a desire that their musical activities – and in particular their potential to spread the Christian message to secular metal audiences – would be more openly acknowledged within the wider Finnish Christian milieu. They are, however, less concerned with highlighting Christian metal's legitimacy and less inclined to represent Christian metal as an alternative to secular metal. This is because only a few of them have actually had to repeatedly defend their choice of music over longer periods of time within their own churches. Generally speaking, Finnish Christian churches' attitudes towards extreme musical forms such as metal have become increasingly accepting since the mid-1990s. This also no doubt has to do with metal's highly prominent and visible position within the Finnish popular cultural mainstream (Moberg 2009a: 258–60).

It is important to note that this also has important bearings on the *religious* meanings and functions that many Finnish Christian metal musicians attach to their own musical activities as well as to participating in the scene itself. For many, the practice of making and playing music constitutes an additional avenue through which everyday personal and faith-related issues can be worked out. For its core members, the scene also constitutes a distinct cultural space – both Christian and popular – in which they can share their passion for metal and its particular cultural identity with like-minded people who also share their Christian beliefs (Moberg 2009a: 271).

The establishment of the online forum 'Kristillinen metalliunioni' has provided the Finnish scene as a whole with a central shared channel for information, discussion and debate. Scene members living in the Helsinki metropolitan area and nearby towns also gather regularly in Helsinki for so-called 'cell meetings'. During these meetings scene members not only convene to discuss issues relating to the scene but also to discuss faith-related issues and to pray together. This is a good example of the scene having developed practices that are clearly designed to deepen a sense of community among its members. Scene members from other parts of the country also regularly hear of these meetings, as they are announced through Kristillinen metalliunioni. Importantly, when the scene takes on functions with a direct relation to scene members' everyday religious lives, it does so in a particular popular cultural way that is very different from more traditional modes of expressing and practising Christian faith. The scene should thus be understood primarily as a space in which Christians who are into metal can express their faith in an alternative and complementary way that is fully in line with their cultural sensibilities. This makes it possible to describe the metal scene in terms of a cross-denominational religious community characterised by a set of shared aims and concerns. But, importantly, it is not only scene members' religious views but, to an equal extent also their shared passion for metal, that draws them together. It is thus rather questionable whether the Christian metal scene should really be viewed as a religious community in the full sense of the word. Its peculiar character as a Christian metal *music* scene puts it somewhere on the borderline between a popular music culture and a religious community (Moberg 2009a: 275, 280–82).

As mentioned above, the international Christian metal scene has grown significantly in recent years. The development of the Internet has also greatly aided and speeded up communication between national and regional scenes in different parts of the world. On an international level, the Christian metal scene could thus also be understood in terms of a broader *movement* aimed at cultivating a particular popular-music-inspired alternative and complementary form of religious expression and evangelism. We should note, however, that when described as a movement, the Christian metal scene should not be understood in terms of a movement that is aimed at cultivating any specific Christian teachings. Instead, the scene is expressly constructed as a distinct space aimed at cultivating a particular way of expressing and spreading a broadly defined 'basic' Protestant faith. The Finnish national scene is also characterised by these same broad aims and concerns. By constituting a part of a wider international scene it also provides its members with a sense of being part of a wider international community or movement. However, most musicians confine their activities to the Finnish national scene (Moberg 2009a: 275–6).

As argued by many social theorists, in contemporary late-modern society and culture, identities have become increasingly fluid and reflexive.[9] In particular, identities have become increasingly *chosen* rather than ascribed or imposed. This is equally true of religious identities. As people increasingly, so to speak, have no choice but to choose who they want to be, this may mean that they feel increasingly uncertain about who they are, who they want to be, or who they should be. This has important implications for issues pertaining to religion and religious life in late-modern Western societies. As noted above, in the contemporary Western religious landscape there is an increasing emphasis on individuals choosing, or 'choosing not to choose', their religious or spiritual beliefs and identities for themselves.[10] Viewed in this light, the Christian metal scene could be seen as providing its members with resources for the shaping of an alternative Christian identity and an alternative way of 'doing' religion. Importantly, Christian metal scene members' identities as Christian metalheads are constantly reproduced on an everyday basis and thus become integrated as important parts of their day-to-day lives. It should also be pointed out here that this alternative religious identity is a consciously *chosen* one. As pointed out by Chris Weedon, particular types of identities, such as religious identities, often involve 'active processes of identification' (Weedon 2004: 7). Moreover, as Weedon points out, they may also involve a 'conscious counter-identification against institutionally and socially assigned identities, and the meanings and values that they are seen to represent' (ibid.).

As noted above, within the international scene as a whole Christian metal is discursively constructed as an unconventional form of Christian activity that takes place both on the sidelines of traditional church activity as well as on the borderline between religion and popular culture. The scene provides its members with a space in which this particular alternative form of religious expression and evangelism can be realised in real life and thereby be lived out with like-minded people who share these same concerns. Within the context of their own churches, Christian metalheads represent innovation and renewal in their form of religious expression. However, the alternative *way* of being a Christian and of 'doing religion' that the scene provides to its members also becomes largely detached from any particular Christian institution. Considering its cross-denominational and ecumenical character, the scene as a whole can thus also be seen as functioning as an alternative or complement to a whole range of other more traditional Christian practices. However, this 'alternativeness' should not be overstated. It would a mistake to argue that the Christian metal scene stands in some form of opposition to more traditional church practices. But the scene does allow its members to express their religious beliefs in an alternative and complementary way that is fully in line with their cultural tastes and sensibilities. The main conclusion one can draw is that, on both an international as well as Finnish national level, Christian metal is not about revising or developing new understandings of Christian beliefs, teachings, values or the like. Instead, it is all about cultivating a particular alternative way of expressing and spreading 'basic', conventional and traditional beliefs and values and creating a distinct space in which this can be done together with like-minded people who share the same particular cultural sensibilities (Moberg 2009a: 278–82).

Concluding observations

The Christian metal scene can be seen as reflecting a more widespread need for renewal and greater openness to alternative musical forms within church settings in Finland. Such calls are in themselves nothing new. Above all, it can be taken to reflect a more widespread and growing need among young Christians to be able to express their faith in ways that are more in line with their cultural sensibilities. Of course, the spreading of such attitudes and ideas has been known to students of religion in Finland for quite some time. If the Christian metal scene illustrates anything in particular, it is that there also may be a more widespread need among young adult Christians in Finland today to express their faith in ways that are intimately connected with their popular cultural tastes and the particular cultural identities that go with them (ibid.: 288).

As discussed above, popular culture has come to play an ever more important role in the dissemination of a wide range of alternative religious/spiritual ideas. Indeed, as argued by many scholars of contemporary religion, and also illustrated by the Christian metal scene, particular popular cultural forms may even come to play a formative and determinative role in the religious and spiritual lives of certain groups of people. As argued by Andy Bennett, popular music in particular has come to constitute an ever more important resource for the shaping of personal and cultural identities for increasing numbers of people today (Bennett 2001: 1). The Christian metal scene may thus also reflect a more widespread need for young adult Christians to be able to express their faith within alternative environments that are more directly connected to the broader popular cultural milieu in which they live. As such, it may also be seen as reflecting a more widespread search for new types of Christian identities. In this regard, the Finnish Christian metal scene constitutes a very rare example of a particular group of people actually forming an alternative community of their own in which such needs can be met. However, as noted above, this is not a community that is directed *against* traditional forms of church practice, but is instead expressly represented as offering an *alternative* or *complement* to them. One could thus perhaps also interpret the Christian metal scene as reflecting a more widespread need among young Christians to express their faith in a form and environment of their own choosing. However, one might also question these presumptions since the Christian metal scene is the only alternative popular music-based alternative Christian community to have developed on any scale in Finland so far. It can, however, perhaps be seen as hinting at possible future developments in this regard (Moberg 2009a: 288–91).

In relation to this we also need to note that the Christian metal scene is also about embracing a particular kind of style and look, and in a certain sense, about adopting a certain kind of lifestyle as well. As such, it can be described as a space which allows, and indeed encourages, Christians to express their individuality and 'be themselves'. The scene can thus also be viewed in direct relation to the increasing emphasis on the individual in modern Western society and culture and be taken to reflect a growing need among young Christians to engage with faith in ways that suit their personal tastes and individual needs. This would also be in line with the increasing privatisation of Finnish religiosity. It would, however, also elaborate further on the issue of privatisation by suggesting an increasing privatisation regarding forms of religious expression as well. However, these remain largely tentative observations. In order to be able to say something more certain about these issues, the Christian metal scene would need to be compared with other Christian groups in whose practices some particular popular cultural form occupies a central role. More research focusing on how popular cultural forms increasingly figure within more traditional and institutional religious settings as well is thus called for. As popular culture as a whole has come to play an ever more important role in the religious/spiritual lives of increasing numbers of people, it is clear that Christians are as much a part of these developments as anyone else (ibid.: 288–93).

3

Shout to the Lord

Christian worship music as popular culture, church music, and lifestyle

Thomas Bossius

Throughout history music and religion have walked hand in hand. In the religious rituals of almost all religions, different types of music are used to express faith, to praise the gods and to help believers to experience and make contact with the divine. One special and very ancient type of religious song is the so-called praise or worship song, which is best described as a sung prayer to the god or gods in which the worshipper believes.

Sung worship of this type is found in several religions, and is by no means limited to the cultural sphere of Christianity. Neither is it limited to any particular kind of Christianity; instead it is a central and original practice within all kinds of directions, denominations and movements (*Pilgrim* 2001). This chapter does not deal with praise and worship music in a broader cultural or historical perspective, however. Instead the focus is on the development that has taken place in this area in the Protestant Free Church Movements during the late twentieth and early twenty-first centuries.

Beginning in the 1970s, Christian worship music developed from one song category among others to one of the most dominant genres in the contemporary Christian music scene. Worship music gained a growing following and a more central position among young Christians, acquired a more modern popular musical expression, had a considerable influence on church music, and, at least for the most devoted, developed into a lifestyle.

Musically, most of the new worship music is based on the styles and sounds of pop, rock, country and soul, but also other types of music are used. Christian popular music in these genres is far from new. It has existed since at least the middle of the 1960s (Bossius 2005). Nor are praise and worship lyrics connected to these types of music anything new, but are rather to be considered as standard lyrical genres in Christian popular music ever since it began in the 1960s.

What is specific and new about contemporary worship music is instead that, despite its close relationship to the mentioned genres, it does not function primarily as popular music, but as sacred devotional music. Worship music is not performed as entertainment, but as prayer music in ordinary services or special worship services. In addition, worship concerts are also arranged. These concerts can be said to be something between a worship service and a rock concert. The character of these concerts differs according to what age group they are directed at. If the concert is aimed at an adult or mixed audience, it usually has more the character of a prayer meeting than a rock concert. At more youth-oriented worship concerts on the other hand, the line between rock and roll entertainment and worship, at least during the up-tempo songs, becomes very thin. And some of these concerts, at least when seen on DVD, give the impression of being more like conventional rock concerts than prayer and worship meetings.

At both the worship services and the worship concerts, however, traditional elements of the church service are mixed with elements from the popular music concert culture, and the musical event in worship culture is an interesting mixture or fusion between a popular music concert and a Christian service. It could be said that the contemporary Christian worship movement positions itself in a liminal space between popular and church culture.

A fact that clearly links worship culture and popular culture is that the worship culture to a large degree documents and spreads itself with the help of commercially produced mass media like CDs and DVDs, videos and Internet, in a way that is completely in line with how the secular popular music industry operates. Apart from the purely commercial media products, there is however also an extensive production of educational materials on worship in the form of CDs and DVDs, videos, websites, sheet music, magazines and books. These products are also sold for a profit, but they are not primarily directed towards an open commercial market. Instead they are directed towards the worship leaders of the congregations, and are marketed not as commercial commodities, but as 'worship resources'.

These resources are often available as subscriptions where three or four times a year subscribers receive a whole package consisting of a CD with new songs, sheet music, and educational materials like a magazine or a book. In addition, different kinds of media also play an important part in the performance of worship. Worship culture can therefore, in several respects, be said to be a media-dense culture.

The aim of this chapter is to describe and analyse the new worship music and culture, and its functions as devotional music, popular culture and lifestyle. It starts with a short historical overview, followed by a description of the worship music and its lyrics. The uses and functions of media in worship culture are then discussed in detail. The chapter ends by considering how the participants view their music, and how worship functions as a lifestyle.

A short history

What today can be described as a global and vivid worship culture started in a modest way in the early 1970s. In the 1990s it went through a development that was so explosive and far-reaching that it is sometimes described as a 'worship revolution' (Zschech 2002: 12). The American theologian Robert E. Webber argues that:

> One of the most controversial revolutions in the church has been the recent changes in worship. Between 1900 and 1970 most churches had settled into the model of traditional worship handed down in their denomination or fellowship. There was little pressure to change until the music revolution of the fifties, the rise of the hippie movement in the sixties, and the emergence of the Jesus Movement in the seventies. The Jesus Movement, influenced by the music revolution and the hippie revolution, introduced music-driven casual worship, and the church has been in an uproar ever since.

> This genre of 'praise and worship' has become the mark of the contemporary megachurch and the symbol of what attracts and holds the young. (Webber 2002: 187)

Apart from the American Jesus Movement that Webber describes, two other relatively new Free Church Movements should be mentioned as crucial for the emergence and establishment of the contemporary worship music: the American Vineyard Movement and the Australian Hillsong Movement, both of which started in the early 1980s.

The Jesus Movement emerged from the American hippie movement during the early 1970s. Many of the participants were musicians, and music was always a central part of its activities. This music was mainly rock, inspired both by the musicians' roots in hippie culture and by their experience of salvation. Besides the rock music they also developed a kind of soft-voiced, acoustic worship music with musical inspiration taken from older Christian hymns and the American folk-song tradition. They soon also started to merge the worship and the rock music into one, which can be seen as the birth of the new or contemporary worship music. The American theologian Mark Allan Powell states that 'the American contemporary worship movement . . . began with a series of praise albums issued by Maranatha in the '70s and continued with copycat versions from the Vineyard churches that were issued throughout the '90s' (Powell 2003: 748). On the website of Maranatha! Music the early development is described in the following way:

> Maranatha! emerged from the heart of the 'Jesus Movement' in the early 1970s as a voice of hope to a turbulent generation. A grand scale conversion took place in the Christian church as thousands of these 'hippies' found truth and meaning in Jesus Christ as a worldwide spiritual explosion transformed nearly every aspect of the church. People responded with new music out of a heart of worship. This religious cultural revolution, often referred to as the 'Jesus Movement' brought forth a response in song called 'Jesus Music.' Many of these hippie converts, often referred to as 'Jesus People,' congregated at Calvary Chapel of Costa Mesa, pastored by Chuck Smith, Sr. Young Christian musicians who had formed approximately ten bands, began playing their worship music

in Pastor Chuck's church at weekly services and at special concerts purposed on sharing God's love and praising Him. In 1971, with a small loan from Chuck Smith, the first album was recorded, distributed by band members and sold at church concerts. [. . .] After experimenting with artist-driven and concept albums in its early years, Maranatha! changed its vision and slowly started to gear its entire product line toward producing worship albums that would facilitate the needs of churches across the world. Along with many event and ministry related recordings, we developed several genre-specific series that have stood the test of time and improved with their progression. [. . .] Perhaps most renowned for its innovation and energy, is Maranatha's own brand of guitar-driven worship, The Praise Band Series. (From Maranatha Music's homepage: http://store.yahoo.com/maranathaweb/ history.html, accessed on 9 August 2008)

That the records of Maranatha! Music and the Vineyard Movement sounded alike, as Powell states, is far from surprising since Vineyard, like Maranatha! Music, to a large degree developed out of the Jesus Movement. Vineyard's musical style as well as many of the early musicians had their roots in that movement (Croasmun 2005: 16). Vineyard, like the Jesus Movement before them, concentrated on contemporary music in their evangelical activities as well as in the services at church. In Vineyard's case the pop- and rock-based worship music was given a larger and growing space, and developed from being above all a mediated form of evangelisation, to becoming their main church music.

The Jesus Movement, Maranatha! Music and the Vineyard Movement were for a long time the great forerunners and renewers of worship music and culture. Lately, their Australian successor Hillsong has more or less taken over the role of the leading worship creators. The origin of Hillsong was in the small Hills Christian Life Centre, founded in Sydney 1983. According to the website of Hillsong the centre's goal was 'to provide people in Sydney's North West with an active, contemporary church', but also to 'reach and influence the world by building a large Bible-based church, changing mindsets and empowering people to lead and impact in every sphere of life' (from Hillsong's homepage: www.hillsong.com, accessed on 9 August 2008).

The Hillsong Movement has been very successful, and has developed from a membership of 45 people into – again according to the group's own website – possibly the largest church in Australia. Today Hillsong is a worldwide Free Church organisation where the Christian gospel is spread not only through traditional Christian teaching, but also with the help of mass media products like CDs, books, films, TV programmes and the Internet. The organisation also arranges large rock concert-like services and music festivals, with the focus on the type of rock and pop-based worship music that has become the Hillsong trademark.

Worship in Sweden

In Sweden the Vineyard Movement has become particularly well established, with several congregations primarily in the larger towns such as Gothenburg and Stockholm. In Sweden, as in other countries, the movement has been very active as music producers. The first congregation in Sweden, Stockholm Vineyard, was established in 1992 by the Baptist pastor Hans Sundberg (Evenbratt 2003: 17). The establishment of Vineyard was an important step in the ongoing development and establishment of the new worship music, but the contemporary praise and worship music and its associated culture had already been strongly rooted in most parts of Sweden for a long time.

It is always difficult to determine the exact time when a cultural phenomenon such as worship music actually arose. When it comes to worship music in Sweden, however, the year 1971 was without doubt of great significance. During summer and fall 1971 a group of representatives of the American Jesus Movement visited Sweden. Led by Lonnie Frisbee, they travelled around Sweden and led several services where they talked about their newfound faith, and sang the new kind of soft-voiced, acoustic worship songs that they themselves had helped develop. A recording made by the Pentecostal Movement's record label Hemmets Härold gives a good indication of how the Jesus People sounded and how they performed their songs. The recording was made live during a late-night service in City Pingstförsamling (the City Pentecostal Congregation) in Stockholm on 26 August 1971. The songs recorded had a great impact on the Swedish Free Church community. They were still being sung long after the broadcast, and inspired the composition of several new songs in the same style.

The EP record featuring the Jesus People was the first Swedish recording of the new worship music. However, since the musicians and singers on that record are all American, the record that is usually counted as the first Swedish worship recording is the LP *En sång, ett folk* ('One Song, One People'), composed and recorded by author Ylva Eggehorn and released by another Pentecostal record label PRIM in 1976. On the sleeve of this record Eggehorn describes her songs and the environment in which they were created. Her description gives a good picture of what worship culture was about, then as well as now:

> This record is mirroring a process. One song, One people. People all over the world have begun to discover each other as brothers and sisters in Christ. Not theoretically but in practical everyday reality. The renewal has been given different names: the Jesus Movement, the Charismatic Revival, the Social Revival. But these are only different expressions for what is being created when we come together as one People of God. And in the joy of that, songs are being born, thousands of songs in different countries which are being spread from mouth to mouth, and often are built on words from the Bible. They are created by ordinary people . . . They are bearing witness of the life that we share with each other as one body in Christ. They are Praise Songs. They are often directly addressed to Him, who has put this new song in us. They are 'Life Songs'. They are often created in times of difficulty as a concrete encouragement for the one who got the song and as a Life Giver for others who get to share it.

Starting in 1979 *En sång, ett folk* was followed by a series of worship records on the PRIM label. The inspiration, as well as some of the songs on these records, was taken from the recordings of Maranatha! Music. The impact and significance of worship were growing with every record. The first Free Church Movement in Sweden that seriously concentrated on using the new worship music in its services was Livets Ord (Word of Life), established in the early 1980s. According to the Swedish music- and song-leader Carina Cederborg, it was then and there that the new praise and worship music was established and began to be spread throughout Sweden. During the second part of the 1980s this trend spread like wildfire. 'In the late eighties', Cederborg says, 'suddenly all churches had to have a worship team and the overhead-sheets had to be put on and the church choirs closed down' (interview with Carina Cederborg, 29 September 2005). The rapid breakthrough seems to have taken many of the churchgoers by surprise, and – again according to Cederborg – caused conflicts and ruptures in many congregations. Since then, however, the development has slowed and the situation has stabilised. Another Swedish musician, Pernilla Thörewik, says in an interview in the Swedish Christian newspaper *Dagen* that church choirs have once again started to flourish (*Dagen* 2004).

Even though the choirs have started to recover, there is no doubt that the new praise and worship music will be around for a very long time. It is now well established both in older congregations and in newer ones where the new type of worship is taken for granted. The 'new' congregations that are centred on worship, like their precursors, focus particularly on young people. They are striving to find both a spoken and a musical language that can attract and be accepted by the young members of contemporary society.

On the website of one such new congregation, NXTchurch, which started in Gothenburg around 2004, the founders write that they want to be 'a next generation church'. To achieve this goal they strive towards a programme that is relevant for young people – adolescents and young adults – and meets them on their own terms. It is the modern, globally connected inhabitants of the big cities they want to reach, and for whom they strive to be relevant. They attempt to be:

> a church that lives in the global metropolitan culture, and understand how it affects us who live in it. Through this, church will communicate the gospel through a time appropriate and attractive method, form, style and structure, and help people to live with Jesus in their everyday situation. (From NXT's homepage: www.churchnxt.se, accessed on 9 August 2008)

In NXTchurch, different media, together with Hillsong-inspired worship, are central features. When the church was launched in 2004, it was done with the help of a website. The website still plays a central role in church activities, featuring advertisements not only for new members, but also for new collaborators who can produce videos, work with sound and light equipment, and lead the worship.

NXTchurch is a typical example of the new type of congregations started by young adults, who target their own and younger generations with the help of pop and rock-based worship music, among other attractions. Another example is the Oslo-based congregation Subchurch, which comprises young Christians whose common interest, besides their Christian faith, is their love for subcultural music and lifestyles, and especially extreme metal. In Subchurch worship music is used as church music, in this case in the form of heavy, guitar-based rock.

The reception of contemporary worship music

The sudden impact of worship music in the 1990s was met with some surprise. 'It is strange', says song-leader Pernilla Thörewik in the interview in *Dagen*, 'suddenly a musical style called worship popped up. As if all songs that are directed towards God are not worship' (*Dagen* 2004). Worship music was received with great enthusiasm during the 1980s, but during the 1990s there was growing criticism of the genre. Most of the voices were not critical of worship in itself, but of the large number of ever-more similar sounding records. The Swedish musicians and producers Jan and Per Nordbring, who have been involved in several Swedish worship recordings, describe the development as follows:

> During the eighties Christian record companies were looking for bands who could break into the secular market as well. It almost became an entertainment industry inside the church. But this Christian pop bubble finally burst, and its death was a form of self-clearance, says Jan. They see the wave of worship music as a reaction to the rather bland Christian music that dominated the 1980s . . . Now the Christian music business hasn't got the same commercial character. Today there's no point in trying to do anything to make money, instead you do things with your heart, says Jan . . . We would never be able to make a living making Christian records, says Per. (*Dagen* 2003c)

Even though they describe 'the wave of worship music' as a reaction to the commercial Christian pop music of the 1980s, later on in the interview these producers voice a common criticism of the development of worship music:

> If one could make a wish it would be that the Christian line of business took a step forward and didn't get stuck in certain frameworks, says Per. As an example they take worship music, where they think that a lot of it sounds the same and isn't challenging . . . Worship has now almost become a musical style of its own. But worship can be all kinds of styles, from classical music to hard rock, says Jan. (ibid.)

As a result of this development, new worship records are often met with a certain amount of suspicion. Two excerpts from reviews in the Swedish Christian youth magazine *Gyro* illustrate this well:

> Worship records can easily become slightly cosmetic: contrived to please and polished for the sake of beauty. Rather often the soul gets lost and the result becomes plastic and boring. Eldkollektivet's[1] record is different . . . This record awakens something inside of me: a longing to seek the situations mentioned above. That's something far from all worship records manage to do. (Jaktlund 2005)

> After having listened to the latest work of Hillsong United, *Look to you*, I start to wonder if I really have got the correct record. Haven't I heard this before? Hillsong is a little bit like McDonald's. You know exactly what you'll get. Boring some would say, safe others would say . . . This is worship that fills me up for the moment, but the risk is that I soon will have overeaten. (Thorstensson 2005)

Eldkollektivet is one of the new voices in the Swedish worship culture that are trying to break the trend of musical one-sidedness within worship, which is warmly welcomed. A good example of this warm welcome can be found in the Christian magazine *Trots Allt* ('After All'), where journalist Tomas Einarsson states that, when listening to Eldkollektivet's first CD *Såsom eld – elden kommer inifrån* ('As Fire – The Fire Comes From Within'; 2002), he does not get 'the same feeling of panic' as he usually does when he listen to worship on record (Einarsson 2002). Einarsson does not seem to dislike worship in itself, only when it is recorded. In an interview with Mia Petersson from Eldkollektivet he asks, 'Is it at all appropriate to release worship on records; is not communal worship something that can only take place in a living congregation?' (ibid.)

Petersson both agrees and disagrees:

> Both yes and no. Worship is needed since God is a god who is worthy of worship. But I am reluctant to give faces and names to the ones involved. When too much industry arises around it, simplicity and freedom are lost. I don't want to be one-sided and reject all worship that comes from England and the USA, but Eld is something else, something less compromising and less contrived. (ibid.)[2]

Music, lyrics, and performance

If one looks at the functions and lyrical content of worship, it can clearly be described as a specific and distinguishable genre. If, on the other hand, one tries to place it within the framework of a specific musical style or genre, one will not succeed. The musical styles of worship music are far too diverse for that. Pop, rock, hard rock, acoustic singer-songwriters, blues, soul, rave and country music can all be found within the ranks of worship. Also, alongside the more modern-sounding music, such things as old psalms, hymns, folk songs, Gregorian chants and songs from the community at Taizé are being used.

While emphasising the diversity of worship music, it must also be stated that most of it – as made clear in the discussion above – is done in a light pop style, with a pure and clear sound, where the lyrics of the song are the main feature. Instrumental sections, shorter solos, and experiments with sound do occur, but never in a way that covers or obscures the vocals. It is always the lyrics and the performance of these that are the main feature and it is the melody of the vocal part that rules the rest.

The melody of the vocals is in its turn ruled and limited by the function of worship as a commonly sung prayer. The songs must be easy to sing and learn. As a help for the congregation – irrespective of whether it is a worship concert at Hillsong Australia with 20,000 participants, or a moment of worship in a local congregation with 20 participants – overhead or PowerPoint-projected lyrics are used to make sure that everyone can sing along. Typically the lyrics consist of no more than a few short phrases that are repeated several times.

Like the lyrics, the melodies are also sparse and consist of a limited number of musical phrases and a calm, harmonic flow. The music and the melodies are not supposed to draw attention to themselves, not to offer surprises and finesses, but to calmly and quietly bear the song and create a harmonic musical space in which the meditative prayer can take place without being interrupted or disturbed.

Like many others who write about worship, the British worship leader Tim Hughes, in his book *Here I Am to Worship* (2004), emphasises the importance of a continuous and uninterrupted flow of the worship. Neither the music nor the worship team are supposed to draw attention to themselves. Two of the most fundamental conditions for this are first of all that the team members play well together and are in harmony with each other, and second that the performance is well rehearsed and prepared so that the flow never needs to be broken by musicians or singers looking for notes and lyrics among their sheets of music (Hughes 2004: 96ff).

Hughes, like the Swedish freelance musician and Vineyard pastor Lars Ekberg, also stresses the importance of a well thought-through succession of the tunes. The succession should be such as that the tunes that follow each other harmonise in tempo as well as style. 'If the tempo is almost the same in a row of songs', writes Ekberg, 'you won't have to make a break; instead you can continue directly with the next song' (Ekberg 2005). Both Ekberg and Hughes also emphasise the importance of the keys of the songs. If the change of key is too abrupt the flow will be broken. Therefore it is important to ensure that the transition from one key to another is softened by using harmonising keys or well chosen transitional chords that lead over from one key to another (Ekberg 2005: 14; Hughes 2004: 91ff).

To be a worship musician means to keep a low profile artistically. There are several musicians and bands that tour under their own names and perform both as independent artists and as worship leaders. But most of the worship teams and worship leaders bill themselves not as independent artists or bands, but as the worship team of their home congregation whose function is to lead the common worship in the services. Tim Hughes writes:

> Being involved in worship inevitably means being involved with a church. Worship should always be at the heart of any church, and the style and direction will be birthed from the vision of the church as a whole. It's unhealthy for both the musicians and the church if musicians only attend church when they play. It's also unhealthy if the band heads off elsewhere during the sermon, after having led the church in worship. It can present a 'them and us' attitude. It's important that the worship team is involved in the whole service and is part of the church family. (Hughes 2004: 77)

In this there is a clear difference in relation to the individualistic fixation on idols in the world of secular popular music, but also in relation to the more pure Christian popular music culture, which is characterised by bands and musicians with a more free or loose relationship to their home congregations (Bossius 2005: 508ff; Thorsén 1980: 25). Another important difference between popular culture and worship culture is the withdrawn role of the musicians when they perform. It is not the musicians and singers that are supposed to be focused upon and glorified, but God, and the weight and importance of a humble approach and a low profile are strongly and consistently emphasised (Hughes 2004: 35ff; Zschech 2002: 95f, 151ff, 192).

Worship culture: a movement divided in two

The picture painted so far of the Contemporary Worship Movement is that of a unified movement. In reality, however, it is better described as a movement consisting of two parts. One part comprises the mass mediated worship music that is being produced by the commercial Christian media industry. The other part consists of the living praise and worship music that is being practised by communities and individuals without any commercial interests at all. This second part in itself can be broken down into two separate but intertwined practices. On the one hand there are the communally performed songs of praise and worship that are sung in church; on the other hand the individually practised praise and worship that stretches far beyond the borders of song and music and turns into a lifestyle.

In my interview with Carina Cederborg I raised questions concerning the relationship between recorded and live worship music. I asked her if the two were best seen as a connected whole, or as two separate parts.

One thing Cederborg emphasised in her answer was that she, as a worship leader in her church, had nothing to do with the industry around praise and worship music and that she had a very little interest in it. To her, praise and worship music should only be performed and used for a purpose, and her interest in it was entirely focused on its use in the services and the communal experience of God. To the direct question whether recorded and live worship could be seen as two separate things she answered:

> That's a hard question to answer; you can't deny that praise and worship has become a musical compartment in the record shelves, because it has. But here in our church we try to move away from that compartment, that it's about a certain type of music, and instead point to the fact that it is a way of life, to live turned towards God . . . it's not about singing, it's about worshipping God. (Cederborg 2005)

The only direct connection Cederborg could see between herself and the worship industry was that she and other worship leaders search for inspiration and new songs from the records and the sheet books.

The role of media in worship culture

If you approach worship culture by means of the mass-produced media products, you can easily get the impression that worship culture is balancing between the commercial popular culture and the non-commercial culture of the Christian service. However, as Cederborg's description shows, the commercial culture is no threat to the living praise and worship culture. For those who, on the other hand, have an investment in making a living from and spreading praise and worship music with the help of media products, the commercial culture is an ever-present danger that must be guarded against. This is because key agents in the scene believe that if commercial forces make a total breakthrough and take over, then the record-producing worship leaders would turn into pop artists, and their worship music would lose most of its power and meaning. An example of this point of view is given by the editor of the *Lovsång* magazine, Lars Petersson, in one of his editorials:

> There is nothing wrong with Michael W. Smith, but to be honest it was more of a sing-along with Kjell Lönnå than a moment of worship.[3] On GMA Week the most important thing is who is leading the worship not the actual worship. The concept 'worship' is still hard currency and an obvious trend is that artists make at least one worship album in their career . . . The records are freely and easily marketed in the same way as any pop record. The market forces are squeezing the essence out of worship and I end up becoming immune to all 'praise God' delivered to me, because the actual message is 'see me, love me, buy my record'. (Petersson 2005)

To counteract this commercialisation, educational material is also produced explaining the 'proper way' to use worship. The proper way, according to these sources, is not to spread the worship music as popular music, but to protect its function as worship and devotion.

In worship culture, as in the Free Church movements in general, there is an obvious ambivalence towards the commercial media industry. A good example of this can be found in Tim Hughes's mixed feelings about the success of worship music:

> In many ways worship music has become an industry. Many predict that in the coming years it will become the dominant genre in Christian music worldwide. There has been an explosion in the number of songs, CDs, DVDs, websites and books that are now dedicated to this worship movement. I think it's wonderful to see such a release of creativity; the wealth of resources can only be a blessing to the Church. However, in the midst of it all, I sometimes feel a bit uncomfortable. As worship leaders, are we getting too preoccupied with the sounds and songs we are creating? Is there a danger that we look first and foremost at gifting and talents and forget the key thing – the heart? (Hughes 2004: 28f)

Lars Petersson, like Tim Hughes, has a conflicted relationship with the record industry and the commercial potential of worship music. Hughes is a worship leader in a congregation, but also a songwriter and recording artist. Petersson puts himself in opposition to the commercialisation of worship, but has at the same time – in his capacity as owner of David Media, the leading label for worship music in Sweden – a vested commercial interest in the phenomenon. Every year David Media releases and distributes a vast number of worship records on CD and DVD. In addition to the music records David Media also publishes educational materials on worship in the form of sheet music, books, magazines, CDs and DVDs.

The statement that the worship records are being produced with a commercial purpose should, however, at least in the case of the Swedish market, be taken with a pinch of salt. Christian music sells in small amounts and there are no big fortunes to be made in that sector of the music business. The promoted agenda of the record labels is that their main motivation is to spread the faith, rather than make money.

That praise and worship records in their best moments can fill this function is clearly shown in Benjamin Pålsson's review of the CD *Bara hos Dig. Live från Livets Ord – Youth* ('Only with You. Live From the Word of Life – Youth'; 2005). Pålsson writes:

> This was for me a longed-for record release, and I'm really pleased. A genuine love for Jesus and a passion for Him shine throughout the whole record . . . For me this CD is a good support for praise and worship in my everyday life, you get happy and are filled with gratitude and joy to Jesus! A direct hit! (Pålsson 2005)

Hence, while on one level commercial recordings are the primary expression of worship culture, for those who actively take part in worship, the commercial product has little to do with worship culture. Not only this, but – as Lars Petersson pointed out – the recordings can in a sense be seen as worship's worst enemy if market powers squeeze the essence out of worship and turn it into meaningless community singing (Petersson 2005). Singing a series of worship songs headed by a well-known worship artist is just not enough to make it actual and true worship.

The view on music and worship as a lifestyle

According to the active worshippers, worship in the true sense is something completely different from, and much more than, just some nicely packaged catchy pop tunes on a CD, or a moment of communal singing in church. Carina Cederborg writes that 'praise and worship' have nothing to do with music at all, 'instead it's about our hearts movement towards God's heart, where we let His thoughts become our thoughts and His will become our will' (Cederborg 2003: 4); and in an interview in *Dagen* the Swedish worship musician and composer Bengt Johansson says that 'The immediate and glorious thing about worship is that it is a kind of prayer and direct contact with the powers of heaven' (Johansson 2003).

This description of devoted praise and worship as a lifestyle and an ideal is common to all the sources I have come across. But what does this lifestyle consist of, and how does it express itself? Bengt Johansson says that to him:

> worship as a lifestyle is about living turned towards God. Even in the dark hours of life to shout to him . . . It also means turning away, all the time, from your anger, bitterness, and envy – to make yourself a living sacrifice . . . and to show who God is and the character of God, in what he has done in my life, but also the wrestling and struggle . . . That is the heart of worship – to live turned towards God even in lament. (Johansson 2003)

To have praise and worship as a lifestyle does not mean that you now and then unite with your fellow believers in song, but that you 'worship God with your life' (Cederborg and Mattson 2003). This, they say:

> is maybe the hardest thing to do. It's about putting all of your 24-hours-a-day-7-days-a-week-life at God's disposal. It's a lifestyle . . . When God is at the centre of somebody's heart her life will be transformed from within and shaped into the likeness of Christ. When God is at the centre of somebody's heart she will want to tell others about Jesus. When God is at the centre of somebody's heart she will receive God's heart for other people who suffer. Worship does not make us

detached from the world or self-absorbed; it makes us God-attached and absorbed in the needs of other people!

In my interview Cederborg described it as follows, if you are living in praise and worship, all you do becomes part of your worship. The way you meet, treat and speak to your fellow humans 'is all a part of your worship' (Cederborg 2005).

Praise and worship are not described as any kind of constructed lifestyle, but as something existentially fundamental and necessary in our lives. The meaning and reason of life is said to be accommodated in worship. We are created to worship, and a lack of worship leads to a lack in our lives:

> Worship is our highest calling. There is nothing of more importance that we can do in this life . . . That is what we have been created for. We have been designed by God for this sole purpose. It is our duty and joy to worship . . . Singing songs to God isn't enough; that in itself is not worship. Worship involves offering to God all that we are and all that we'll be – offering our heart, soul and mind. (Hughes 2004: 21f)

> More and more people have discovered that WORSHIP is a necessity of life . . . We see that worship, its musical and lyrical simplicity aside, has an enormous power. God's resources are set free in our lives and through us He can then work. We are disarmed of all egoism, envy, indifference, and become unselfish, both towards each other and God. We are changed not only as individuals but also as congregation – we become united. God wants to meet his children, and through worship we put our lives at the service of the Lord, and He sets his people in motion. When you meet Him in praise and worship walls are broken down and new ways are opened for you. (Sandwall 1981)

The Swedish worship leader Madeleine Wallgren gives the same description. Those who start to worship, she writes, will find that worship raises them above the limitations of everyday life, and let them enter 'the world of the spirit, the world of possibilities. What until

then seemed hopeless and like a heavy burden, is no longer a problem'
(Wallgren 2000: 17).

Peter Sandwall mentions that praise and worship music 'has an
enormous power', and this is another frequent theme in the descriptions that are given of praise and worship. On the cover of the LP
Öppnade ögon ('Opened Eyes'; 1979), worship is described as songs of
joy and praise, but also as 'a weapon in the struggle against the enemy'.
When God's people are united in 'true worship' the evil powers must
yield and flee, they write. In a similar vein Darlene Zschech describes
worship as a direct war against the powers of evil:

> When we, God's people, come into His presence with thanks-
> giving and praise, warfare is waged against our enemies, and
> our battles are won by the supernatural power of God. In
> the face of challenge and persecution, God's people are to
> unite and praise Him. The Enemy has no chance of winning
> against people who are consumed with praising God. There is
> no victory against those who rejoice in God's great glory . . .
> Praise is not a 'happy-clappy' song. Praise is not the fast songs
> before the nice, slow worship songs. Praise is a declaration, a
> victory cry, proclaiming faith to stand firm in the place God
> has given you. Praise is proclamation that the Enemy's intent
> to plunder you will not rock you. Praise declares that you will
> not be moved by the Enemy's attempt to snatch you away . . .
> Praise takes you into the presence of God where the Enemy
> has no choice but to flee. (Zschech 2002: 52f)

The soft-voiced and finely tuned songs of worship are then seen by
their singers as something far more powerful and something much more
than just a series of nice songs. Worship is claimed to be the reason for
our existence and the meaning of our lives, but it is also a source of
strength and a protection against the threatening surrounding world.
This source of power is not seen as limited to the actual moments of
worship singing, but as something that will guide you 24 hours a day
for the rest of your life. This is why several of the active participants
in worship culture talk about worship as a lifestyle. Worship is not just
seen as a type of music, but as a way of life, a way of viewing one's own
existence, and a way to look upon and relate to God.

Summary

The best way to see contemporary worship culture is as a single movement consisting of two parts. One part consists of mass mediated worship music produced by a commercial Christian media industry, and the other part consists of living praise and worship practised by congregations and individuals with no commercial interests whatsoever.

The mass mediated part is constantly balancing between the commercial popular culture and the non-commercial church culture. The worship music is to a large degree marketed and distributed with the help of modern commercial media, and can in a sense be said to be a media-borne and media-based culture fully comparable with any number of other music cultures in late-modern society. The actual worship culture, however, does not take place on CDs or DVDs, and cannot be captured on any such media.

For the active participants of worship culture, praise and worship are a lifestyle characterised by shifting attention away from yourself, away from the individual, away from your own personal interests. Worship is described as an active way of stepping away from the individualisation and the focus on self-realisation that is said to characterise contemporary society. In worship you instead turn your attention towards God. Worship, then, is seen as something personal and communal at the same time. You enter worship as an individual, but through worship you are united into 'one people of God' (Zschech 2002; Sandwall 1981).

When one speaks of worship as a lifestyle, then, it is not to be seen as a common music taste or external personal style, as is most often the case when the combination of music and lifestyle in late-modern society is put into focus. Instead, worship is to be seen as a common way of looking upon yourself, upon the Christian life, upon God, and upon the surrounding contemporary existence. With the help of praise and worship, the participants of worship culture turn away from the alienating, threatening, secularised and splintered surrounding world, and seek nearness to the God they put their trust in. In that way they collect the strength they need to face the challenges and problems that confront them in contemporary late-modern society.

4

Jews United and Divided by Music

Contemporary Jewish music in the UK and America[1]

Keith Kahn-Harris

As twin pillars of the 'West', Europe and America are important points of comparison in the study of contemporary industrialised society. This has never been truer than with regard to the study of religion. In recent years, assumptions about the 'secularisation' of the West have given way to a more complex understanding of how the role of religion in society has been transformed in different locations in different ways. For Grace Davie (2002) Western Europeans[2] broadly speaking 'believe but do not belong' – they are 'unchurched' – whereas Americans are much more inclined to be religiously 'seeking' and 'consumerist'. There are clearly many nuances that complicate any simple picture of European–American contrasts (see for example Halman 2006; Voas 2005). There is significant 'religious consumerism' in Europe as well as in America. Similarly, there are plenty of Americans who 'believe without belonging'. Furthermore, when one broadens the spectrum of religious practice to include non-Christian religions, the picture becomes even more opaque. Nonetheless, in a globalised world, Europe and America can be viewed as providing distinctly different religious models.

Different models of modernity do not emerge in isolation from one another, but are moulded through complicated global networks of communication. Members of religions throughout the world are in communication with each other, and global religious institutions create connections between religious practitioners in different locations. The global religious landscape is one of fragmentation and of unification – of difference and of homogeneity. The same is true for other global social and cultural phenomena that, to varying degrees, produce both global fragmentation and unification. One of the most important forms of global cultural expression is that of popular music. As a central part of the global entertainment industry, popular music is closely implicated in processes through which cultural forms, often originating in America and the 'Western' world, are globally disseminated. This process is highly uneven and the situation is far from a case of 'one-way traffic'. Western popular music is not equally successful in all parts of the world; Western forms are adapted in idiosyncratic ways in local contexts; non-Western forms are also disseminated in the west (Lipsitz 1994; Mitchell 1996; Taylor 1997; Born and Hesmondhalgh 2000).

An examination of the interaction of popular music and religion sheds light on the interplay between two forces of global fragmentation and unification. Looking at how religious communities in one location draw on popular music from another location provides an insight into the ways in which religion is positioned in relation to global cultural flows. A consideration of popular music and religion in Europe and America helps to illuminate the complex relationship between these two cultural–religious models.

This chapter considers how one particular form of popular music – contemporary Jewish music – circulates between the British and American Jewish communities. In focusing on how the music of the pioneering contemporary American contemporary Jewish musician Debbie Friedman has been received in Britain, I will consider how contemporary Jewish music both provides a cultural 'bridge' between two Jewish communities and also highlights deep differences between them.

Popular music in the Jewish world

The Jewish world is perhaps a small one (around 13 million in 2005 according to DellaPergola, Dror et al. 2005) but it has historically been a highly globalised one, with significant communities located throughout the world. The holocaust, immigration and assimilation have, however, concentrated the global Jewish population within a small number of significant centres and a larger number of smaller concentrations. Israel and the United States are the main Jewish population centres with over 5 million Jews each. The European Jewish population is much smaller but still significant, with the French (around 500,000) and British (around 300,000) Jewish populations being the largest outside the former Soviet Union.

Since the destruction of the second temple, Jews have seen themselves as a population 'in exile' (*galut*) or as a 'diaspora'. Implicit in both concepts are notions of movement and dispersion. The Jewish world has, over millennia, developed sophisticated practices intended to bind Jews together over considerable expanses of space and time. Texts, individuals and ideas have always circulated throughout the Jewish world creating a unifying sense of being a 'people' (*am*) that has been sustained remarkably successfully despite often trying historical circumstances. At the same time, the process of diaspora creates continuous fissures both between and within Jewish communities scattered throughout the world.

The balance between processes of unification and fragmentation is a delicate one. It is threatened when particular locations within the diaspora become in some way privileged. In the contemporary Jewish world, the disparity in size and wealth between the Israeli and American Jewish communities and other Jewish communities is noteworthy. This disparity means that Israeli and American Jews may have much more influence over the direction of global Jewry than other communities do. Just as is the case with other global cultural flows, the popular music industry included, there are imbalances. Yet at the same time – again as in the popular music industry – there is no straightforward 'cultural imperialism'. Local idiosyncrasy and difference is still retained throughout the spectrum of smaller and more marginal Jewish communities.

Music has been an important marker of difference within world Jewry. There is a vast range of melodies used within the liturgy. Not only are different musical styles and modes preferred in different locations, but different families and peer groups often use different melodies for the same elements of the liturgy. In modernity, this musical anarchy has been both reduced and added to. The growth of Jewish umbrella institutions (such as the Reform and Conservative movements in America) meant that certain styles and melodies came to be dominant and in some cases even prescribed. At the same time, the major Jewish population movements of the last two centuries meant that new forms of music were transplanted to new locations where they co-existed and competed with other forms.

The case of Jewish popular music is in certain respects even more complicated. For one thing, the division between 'secular' and 'religious' music is extremely blurred in Judaism. Liturgical music can frequently be considered popular in the truest sense of the word. Nevertheless, there is a case for examining Jewish music that draws on post-1950s African American-derived popular music as a separate field. This is because the engagement by Jews in this kind of music has been paradoxical and complex. Jews have been highly involved in the development of contemporary popular music as performers, songwriters, producers and impresarios, in America and elsewhere (Rogin 1996; Billig 2000; Melnick 2001). Yet they have not generally done so *as Jews*: singing about Jewish themes and openly identifying themselves as Jewish. The development of an openly Jewish popular music, for specific consumption at least in part within the Jewish community, has been highly erratic.

In mapping the landscape of contemporary Jewish popular music, a number of salient points are immediately visible. There is no global Jewish popular music, consumed by Jews throughout the world, that corresponds to other diasporic musics such as the music of various South Asian diasporas or that of African-originated 'black Atlantic' (Gilroy 1993). Jewish popular music is not commercially important, with the partial exception of klezmer, which has a niche within the 'world music' market (Slobin 2000). A further complicating factor is the position of the thriving Israeli popular music industry, which produces music by Jews in Hebrew yet has a very limited market amongst Jews outside Israel (Regev and Seroussi 2004). There are Jewish popular musics that bind different communities together, but they tend to be the popular musics of particular kinds of Jews. Ultra-Orthodox Jews have their own extremely vital popular music industry that constitutes a truly global culture. Zionist groups, particularly Zionist youth movements, also have a distinctive popular music culture (ironically, one increasingly seen as archaic in Israel itself).

Compared with the high level of development of Jewish liturgical music, Jewish popular music is not a strong force for either unification or fragmentation within the Jewish world. Rather, Jewish popular music reveals the fissures within the Jewish world and the limitations of diasporic cultural flows. The case study of contemporary Jewish music will demonstrate this.

Debbie Friedman and the American contemporary Jewish music scene

The United States boasts the most extensive range of Jewish musical communities in the Jewish world. With the partial exception of klezmer, most American Jewish music is produced and consumed outside the non-Jewish mainstream of the music industry. This is just as true for Jewish popular music that draws on and contributes to the legacy of post-1950s African American derived music. There are two broad modes of relating to contemporary popular music: ethnic and religious. The former consists of music such as klezmer that deals with non-religious themes, is often played by secular Jews and is primarily concerned with establishing and exploring Jewish ethnic difference (including internal ethnic difference). Religious Jewish music is music that, at some level, foregrounds the belief, theology and ritual practice at the heart of its version of Jewishness. Generally speaking, the ethnic mode tends towards a syncretic relationship to popular music – in which Jewish musical sources are combined in various ways with non-Jewish ones – and the religious mode tends towards an appropriative relationship – in which non-Jewish music is drawn on as a vehicle for a Jewish 'message'.

Whilst there are many exceptions to these rules, the case study of the contemporary Jewish music scene demonstrates the generally appropriative mode of religious Jewish popular music. Contemporary Jewish music (CJM) is the term often applied to forms of American Jewish popular music that have developed since the 1960s; that emerged principally from the Reform and Conservative movements;

that frequently use English lyrics and that borrow extensively from a restricted set of contemporary popular music styles.

The strain of contemporary Jewish music that I am particularly interested in is that which emerged in the 1960s via the medium of Reform Jewish summer camps. Summer camps have been a part of diaspora Jewish life since the early twentieth century. This is particularly true of the United States where summer camps are a standard part of the middle-class American youth experience. Jewish summer camps draw to varying degrees on a number of historical antecedents, such as the Zionist youth movement, the scout movement, Christian youth movements and German outdoors movements. The importance of camping in the American Reform Jewish world grew in the post-war period. Summer camps are intended to provide an intense experience of Jewish practice that will hopefully lead to greater Jewish identification (particularly with the Reform movement) during the rest of the year.

From the beginning, singing and song-leading have been important parts of American Reform Jewish summer camping (Schachet-Briskin 1996). As Cohen (2006: 194) puts it: 'Through its centralized placement, songleading . . . became an emblem of the Reform Jewish camp experience itself.' Communal singing occurs not only at special song sessions, but also at synagogue services, mealtimes and countless informal occasions. The focus is on singing accompanied by the guitar, which, as Cohen argues, 'served as a dominant icon for representing music and musical leadership at camp' (Cohen 2006: 196). Although there is a strong ethic of equal participation, and formal musical training is not required, song-leading is a practice that is actively taught. To this end, camps have offered specialised song-leader training at certain camps since the 1960s, and 'Hava NaShira', a specialised song-leader camp, was established in the 1990s. Such training is inseparable from the training of Reform Jewish leaders, as song-leading is a prestigious route into communal leadership positions.

At camp, singing takes place in a number of contexts ranging from the liturgical to the avowedly non-liturgical. Nevertheless, the difference between the repertoires used in such contexts is not clear cut and there is no absolute separation between liturgical and non-liturgical music, still less between sacred and profane. The *Shironim* (songbooks) that have been produced over the years reflect this in their diversity. Zionist pioneer songs coexist with 'traditional' melodies, with liturgical and biblical texts reset with modern tunes, and with English-language popular music. The latter is a particularly striking feature of camp music, with 1950s/60s American folk music by the likes of Joan Baez, Simon and Garfunkel, and Peter, Paul and Mary being particularly influential, along with modern tunes by bands such as the Dave Matthews Band. Whilst the repertoire of Reform Jewish summer camps has never been static, a recognisable style has emerged that harks back to the values and aesthetics of 1960s folk music and hippiedom.

This style has also engendered a large and growing core of music written within and emerging from the camp experience. Since the 1960s, the musical cultural of American Reform Jewish camping has spread, first to NFTY (North American Federation of Temple Youth, the Reform Jewish youth movement), then to Reform synagogues, and then onward to the wider Jewish scene. By the 1990s, music by camp alumni had made substantial inroads into synagogue liturgy. This process has been uneven, varying from synagogue to synagogue, and has encountered substantial resistance, particularly among the more traditionally minded cantors. Today, graduates of the Reform cantorial college routinely learn song-leading and guitar-playing as part of their study programme. Songs developed and popularised at camps form an increasingly well-established part of the liturgy. This includes both new tunes to traditional sections of the liturgy as well as new songs, including songs written both in English and Hebrew.

Particularly important in this process has been Debbie Friedman.[3] Debbie Friedman was born in 1952 in New York state, but grew up in Minnesota, an area with a small Jewish population (an interesting echo of Bob Dylan). She was a product of the summer camp system and learned song-leading and the guitar within it (despite not being able to read music). She maintains a strong connection to the Reform camp system of the 1960s:[4]

> I am a product of the Reform youth system . . . It was a wonderful wonderful movement. It was a movement concerned with social action and a movement concerned with human values. And they were tied to Torah. And it was value-oriented. And it connected every nerd in the world!

They weren't such nerds; they were wonderful people and they really cared about the world and transforming the world and we felt we could to affect some change . . . It was very 60s.

These 'very 1960s' values are still at the core of what Friedman teaches:

I still maintain those values. I haven't lost that direction. I haven't lost those things for which we gathered, for which we stood in the 60s. Those values are probably only the staying values, these are two values that nobody can take away. Even though people say that it's really dippy to talk about peace and love, oh people say it's really simplistic . . . but in essence those are two values that nobody can degrade, nobody can deny you the right to feel those feelings.

By the early 1970s Friedman was writing, and later recording, her own music that quickly became added to the camp repertoire. While Friedman was by no means the first or the last to follow this route (others include Jeff Klepper), she is distinguished by her ongoing popularity, which has grown among American Jewry. Friedman is today the best-known and most successful CJM artist, and in this respect her story is not a typical one within the Reform Jewish camping milieu. At the same time, her story dramatically illustrates the process by which the musical developed in Reform Jewish summer camps has become an important part of the American Reform Jewish world and beyond.

Friedman's body of work consists of 19 albums and a number of song books. Her work has frequently been educationally focused; she has worked in schools and continues to lead choirs and teach song-leading. At the same time, her CDs and concerts are part of a growing set of institutions that constitute the contemporary Jewish music scene. She has toured since the early 1970s and her audience has become broader, moving from camps to synagogues to cross-communal institutions such as Jewish Community Centres. Her status as a popular Jewish artist was cemented in 1996 when she played a 25th anniversary concert at Carnegie Hall, New York. Outside the Orthodox world, where females are not allowed to sing for male audiences, her work has become a part of the Jewish communal landscape in America.

Friedman's work is strongly connected to traditional Jewish texts. She has contributed dozens of new tunes for well-known and less-known passages in the *Siddur* (prayer book) and other Jewish texts such as the *Tanach* (Old Testament). She has also adapted such texts in songs in Hebrew, English or a mixture of both. One of her best-loved songs is 'Not By Might'. Based on a lyric from Zechariah 4:6, it is set to an up-tempo tune that is ideally suited for singing along and is a firm standard within camps and youth movements:

> Not by might, & not by power,
> But by spirit alone
> Shall we all live in peace.
>
> The children sing, the children dream,
> And their tears will fall,
> But we'll hear them call,
> And another song will rise.

One example of her Hebrew-English repertoire is 'Mi Shebeirach' ('The one who blessed'), an adaption of the traditional formula used in blessings:

> Mi shebeirach avoteinu
> M'kor hab'racha l'imoteinu
> May the source of strength,
> Who blessed the ones before us,
> Help us find the courage to make our lives a blessing,
> and let us say, Amen.
>
> [. . .]
>
> Bless those in need of healing with r'fuah sh'leimah,
> The renewal of body, the renewal of spirit,
> And let us say, Amen.

Friedman's version of the prayer uses English to emphasise its healing purpose. 'Mi Shebeirach' has become popular in the American Reform liturgy and is particularly important in healing services. Friedman has helped to popularise healing rituals in the Reform community. She herself has suffered from a severe illness for a number of years and this in part has motivated her to develop new forms of prayer designed to help the healing process. In such ways, Friedman's work has been adopted, with varying degrees of ease, into synagogue services.

Debbie Friedman has also produced work that resembles non-Jewish popular music in more conventional ways, designed to be listened to as much as sung along to. Such songs discuss Jewish issues or more diffuse themes. One example of the former is 'Miriam's Song', which celebrates Moses' sister's life from the perspective of the song she led on crossing the Red Sea:

> Chorus: And the women dancing with their timbrels,
> followed Miriam as she sang her song,
> sing a song to the One whom we've exalted,
> Miriam and the women danced and danced the whole
>   night long.

> And Miriam was a weaver of unique variety
> the tapestry she wove was one which sang our history.
> With every strand and every thread she crafted her delight!
> A woman touched with spirit, she dances toward the light.

Given the educational contexts in which Debbie Friedman's music is used, it is not surprising that a portion of Friedman's work is aimed at children and young people. One such light-hearted song that is also popular with adults is 'The Latke Song' (latkes are potato pancakes eaten on the festival of Chanukah):

> I am so mixed up that I cannot tell you
> I'm sitting in this blender turning brown
> I've made friends with the onions and the flour
> And the cook is scouting oil in town.

> [. . .]

> Chorus: I am a latke, I'm a latke
> And I'm waiting for Chanukah to come.

Friedman resists labelling or categorising her work. In fact, an important feature of her work is its blurring of the boundaries within the Jewish community. Whilst not transgressive in the conventional sense, Debbie Friedman has tried to expand the boundaries of worship within the Jewish community. As she explains about the impact of her early work:

> People were now able to understand prayer, tefilah, in a way that they weren't able to before. We opened doors together . . . to explore the possibility of entering into a level of prayer we had never experienced before together.

As she says about one of her early songs, 'V'ahavta':

> That turned the liturgy upside down . . . that was the first thing I wrote and that was the first thing that kids sang and when they sang it they stood arm in arm, and they were just weeping and it was like all of a sudden they realised that they could take ownership of their tefillah, they could take ownership of what was theirs anyway but they could take it back. They didn't have to use other people's poetry anymore in order to have a meaningful worship experience.

Friedman's work defies any simple division between liturgical and non-liturgical music, although some of her work, such as 'Mi Shebeirach', is particularly well suited to a more ritualistic context. As with contemporary 'worship music' in the Christian context, the distinction between a Debbie Friedman concert and a synagogue service can be a fine one. There is a deliberate attempt to bring prayer out of the synagogue into the world:

> What I'm trying to do is help people to understand that prayer is not limited to the sanctuary or to the synagogue – that prayer is a part of everyday life, part of everyday experience; that it happens in the grocery store as deeply as it happens in the sanctuary. And sometimes it's as vacant in the sanctuary as it can be in the grocery store.

Within the synagogue itself, the use of Friedman's work, and the work of others like her, breaks down the more rigid barriers between the leader of the service and the congregation. Whilst Jews do not have priests, the work of the cantor (*chazan*) often involves very formal (and often quasi-operatic) vocal styles which, particularly if combined with choir and organ, can inhibit participation. The increased popularity of Friedman's work in synagogue services is part of a trend towards greater participation by the congregation in services and a concomitant decline in *chazanut* (solo tunes sung or chanted by the *chazzan*) and classically influenced synagogue art music (Shleifer 1995). This has led to criticism of Friedman and contemporary Jewish music from some quarters, particularly more traditionally minded *chazans*. This controversy is discussed in 'A Journey of Spirit', a 2005 documentary film about Debbie Friedman. However, Friedman herself is not attempting to undermine other approaches to liturgy, asserting that 'A lot of people are really scared that we are going to take their traditional stuff away. I'm not interested in taking anything away from anybody'.

Friedman has also played an important part in the greater participation of women in Jewish ritual life. While Reform Judaism has long preached formal equality of the sexes, only in 1972 were women first ordained as rabbis. Friedman has helped to give women a central role as leaders of worship not simply through her own example but also (as we shall see later in this essay) through her own mentoring activities. Furthermore, Friedman is probably the first woman in Jewish history to have a more than nominal influence on the content of synagogue services.

Friedman's creation of a Jewish analogue to Christian worship music suggests parallels with evangelical Christianity. Inasmuch as Friedman attempts to inspire love of Judaism, that comparison is valid. However, unlike evangelicals, she does not attempt to proselytise amongst non-Jews, nor is she (as some Jewish groups such as Habad are) didactic in encouraging greater Jewish observance. Rather, her work embodies a highly universalist world view:

> It extends beyond Jews; it goes beyond Jewish community to *tikkun olam*,[5] that we have an obligation to conduct ourselves in such a way so as to begin to heal the world and help the world grow and become whole and less chaotic and less pained. That's really what we're here to do, not just a few of us, not just a chosen few but all of us, not just the Jews.

Despite the universalist message of her work, Debbie Friedman has not managed to cross over in any significant way to a non-Jewish market.

Although some of her later albums in particular are less 'Jewish' than her early albums, there does not appear to be an obvious place for her outside the Jewish world. As with contemporary Christian music, contemporary Jewish music circulates in its own world, even if its message may be non-evangelical and potentially universalist. One reason for this may be that Friedman's music, for all its challenging of boundaries in the Jewish world, is very conventional in popular musical terms. Friedman's major innovation has been to change the way music is used in the Reform Jewish community and to challenge the strict demarcations of ritualistic music. However, musically her work is non-innovative and rooted heavily in the music of the 1960s. Although her later work features more complex arrangements and instrumentation, there is little to it that is likely to be of interest to non-Jewish music fans. To put it baldly – there is already a Joan Baez and a Joni Mitchell; why does the world need a Jewish equivalent? This is one of the paradoxes of the work of Debbie Friedman and of other contemporary Jewish musicians: they have had a significant, even radical, effect on elements of Jewish communal and religious practice, while at the same time being musically non-innovative, even perhaps conservative. Contemporary popular music has had a transformative effect on the Jewish community, but the reverse has not been true.

The impact of Debbie Friedman and contemporary Jewish music in the UK

In 1996 I attended the annual Limmud conference that takes place over Christmas every year in Britain. At the welcoming gala, a young British song-leader, Jess Gold, taught the audience a Debbie Friedman song called 'The Time is Now', a song created to be sung at communal events. The song is slow, stately, and emphasises how 'we'll make this space a holy place'. To my surprise, a man in his sixties suddenly got up and walked out, grumbling to his wife that he 'couldn't stand all this pop music'. This incident surprised me as, being accustomed to the more challenging forms of contemporary popular music, I hardly considered that the song might be offensive to anyone. In fact, I myself found the song to be the epitome of consensual music. The incident has stayed with me ever since and has led me to think about how forms of musical innovation – even of the most gentle kind – may cause stress and tensions in the Jewish community. Yet the peeved reaction of the man at the conference is not necessarily typical of the reaction of the UK Jewish community to Debbie Friedman's work. In fact, the very singing of a Friedman song at a large gathering such as Limmud demonstrates how her work has gained a following in the UK.

There are significant international networks through which Jewish leaders from different countries learn from each other. Given its size and degree of organisation, the American Jewish community has always provided inspiration to a steady but significant trickle of British Jewish leaders who visited. The attendance of Reform Jewish youth leaders at summer camps such as Kutz, resulted in American camp music and culture being brought back to Britain. The British Reform youth movement RSY-Netzer (Reform Synagogue Youth: Netzer is a Hebrew acronym for Reform Zionist Youth) has, since the 1960s, developed a Shiron that has strong similarities with the American one. Like their American counterparts, since the 1960s young British Reform Jews have sung a heady mixture of Zionist pioneer songs, traditional melodies and sixties folk and rock n' roll. Since the 1980s, they have been singing Debbie Friedman too. When I attended Reform summer camps in the UK in the mid-1980s, Friedman standards such as 'Not by Might' were among the most popular in the repertoire, and they continue to be popular today.

The entry of contemporary Jewish music into the UK was further facilitated by the growth in popularity of the Limmud conference in the 1990s. Limmud was born in the early 1980s and was originally intended to be a British equivalent of the giant American Coalition on Alternatives in Jewish Education (CAJE) conference. Limmud grew as a cross-communal, anti-establishment challenge to the perceived narrow-mindedness, anti-intellectualism and division of the mainstream Jewish community. By the mid-1990s it drew about 1,000 participants a year, and by the end of the decade this had reached over 2,000. From being a conference for educators it had developed into a diverse showcase of the best of Jewish learning, spawning a strong volunteer culture and attracting speakers and participants from across the world. Music had always been an important part of Limmud since its inception, and since the early 1990s it has invited artists from across the Jewish world. In 1994 Debbie Friedman herself came to Limmud. Her visit to the conference, in which she both performed and directed the Limmud choir, is still talked of today as inspirational. Friedman herself was inspired by her experience at the conference:

> It was one of the most wonderful experiences; I will never forget it in my life . . . It was a very powerful community experience because of it. Everybody was there; everybody showed up; everybody made it beautiful; everybody sang.

Friedman's visit inspired a number of young British Jews to visit America and learn song-leading at American institutions. Ever since Friedman's visit, there has been a steady stream of American contemporary Jewish musicians visiting the conference, such as Rick Recht and Doug Cotler.

However, even if Limmud has provided an important showcase for CJM and for Debbie Friedman, the impact of this music in the UK Jewish community as a whole has been much less than in the American Jewish community. Debbie Friedman and a few others have contributed some repertoire to Jewish youth movements and have played occasional shows in synagogues and other locations.[6] However, contemporary Jewish music has had only a limited impact on the liturgy of Reform and other synagogues. Debbie Friedman tunes are sometimes used, but generally at Friday night services and in services geared towards 'youth' they are far from being mainstream and have not yet challenged the primacy of other forms of liturgical music. Furthermore, there have been few attempts at making a British version of contemporary Jewish music. Inspired by Debbie Friedman, the British song-leader Jess Gold made a CD with her band Red Sea Blue and even toured American summer camps. However, she has been unable to make a living as a song-leader in the UK and her work has not had a wide circulation.

While contemporary Jewish music has had some limited impact in the United Kingdom, there is no contemporary Jewish music 'scene' as such. There are two clusters of explanations for the relatively low presence of CJM in the UK: institutional and cultural. Institutionally, the British Jewish community has a number of crucial differences compared with the American Jewish community. Perhaps the most important is the differing significance of non-Orthodox Judaism. In America, the non-Orthodox denominations (Reform, Orthodox,

Reconstructionalist and others) are in the majority. Of the roughly 40 per cent who are affiliated with a synagogue, around 70 per cent are affiliated with a non-Orthodox synagogue.[7] In the UK, of the 70 per cent of Jews affiliated with a synagogue, around 70 per cent affiliate to a synagogue belonging to an Orthodox umbrella body (Hart and Kafka 2006), although the majority of them are unlikely to be Orthodox in their Jewish practice. The British Reform community, while significant, is a minority, and other non-Orthodox denominations are also small. The non-Orthodox 'power base' of CJM is thus much less significant in the UK than in America.

A further complicating factor in comparing American and British Jewry is that the Reform movements in the two countries do not exactly correspond. While there are institutional connections between the two movements, there are also differences in theology and practice. The British Reform movement has tended to take a slightly more conservative line on Jewish practice and theology. In many ways the British Reform movement tends to correspond to the left-wing of the American Conservative movement (the British Masorti movement corresponds to the right-wing of the American Conservative movement). The American Reform movement tends to correspond more closely to the small British Liberal Jewish movement. All this further fragments the market for CJM in the UK and the possibility of CJM finding a natural 'home' in the UK.

While developed in a non-Orthodox and particularly Reform setting, American CJM is also institutionally supported through cross-communal institutions. The most important of these are Jewish Community Centres, which frequently host concerts in the United States. The UK is only now setting up a Jewish Community Centre in London. CJM artists such as Debbie Friedman are also able to play in cross-communal settings such as the American Jewish Congress. In the UK, the dominance of Orthodox institutions means that cross-communal institutions have to enforce a consensus acceptable to Orthodox members, and this precludes non-Orthodox artists, particularly female artists. Debbie Friedman cannot be a consensual 'common denominator' in the UK. Limmud is one of the very few cross-communal settings in the UK where CJM artists can play.

CJM in the UK also lacks an institutional foothold due to the scarcity of specialist musicians in the community. *Chazans* are much rarer in the UK than in the USA, and there are none working within the Reform community. An important reason for and outcome of the success of Debbie Friedman in the USA was the transformation of the education of *chazans* to include song-leading. It is almost impossible to make a living in the UK as a song-leader or *chazan*, in part because the lack of tradition of this kind of position and in part because of the smaller size of the community. This means that CJM lacks full-time 'champions' who can smooth its entry into the synagogue mainstream.

Over and above these institutional differences between the British and American Jewish communities, there are also cultural differences that have consequences for how CJM has been received in the UK. There are crucial differences between the communities in terms of how Jewish identity is constructed. Cohen and Eisen's study 'The Jew Within' (2000) shows how Jewish identity is constructed in America through the prism of the 'sovereign self'. American Jews tend to search for meaning within Judaism and are inclined to have a consumerist approach to Jewish life. These tendencies help to create a community in which tradition and institutional involvement are less important than finding a way of being Jewish that is personally meaningful. In contrast, research in the UK Jewish community (Cohen and Kahn-Harris 2004) has shown that British Jews are much more committed to ideas of tradition and authenticity than American Jews. Even non-Orthodox Jews in the UK legitimate their Jewish choices more with reference to ideas of correctness and 'properness' than with references to personal meaningfulness. This difference between American and British Jews is reflected in their choices of synagogues; in America there is a much closer 'fit' with the ideology expressed by the synagogue to which Jews are members than in the UK.

CJM foregrounds meaning and spirituality in its vision of Jewish identity. It is earnestly concerned with the individual's spiritual journal and the self's Jewish exploration. In the case of Debbie Friedman's work this is most evident in her emphasis on healing. Established modes of Jewish music practice are less important in CJM than finding a clear and unambiguous vehicle for the communication of 'messages'. There are those within British Jewry who find such a form of Jewish practice attractive. Yet in the main, CJM is a very alien form of Jewish practice in the UK. This is in part due to the heavy use of English. In Orthodox synagogues, English is hardly ever used in prayer, and even in Reform synagogues in the UK (where English prayers are read) few will countenance singing in English. In a community predominantly concerned that Jewish practice should feel somehow authentic and traditional, its use of contemporary modes feels inauthentic. In a community that is less interested in spiritual meaning and personal exploration, CJM's earnestness may feel uncomfortable and even embarrassing. While Limmud concerts by CJM artists do show there is a minority interested in this kind of music, the amount of ridicule they attract from other participants is noteworthy. As the song-leader Jess Gold puts it (personal interview January 2006): 'People don't understand it [CJM] here. It's the whole "happy clappy" thing. People are more into their heads here and they don't like to let go.'

Viewed through the lens of British Jewry, there is much that seems ridiculous in American CJM – its over-earnestness, its dated use of 1960s music, its self-centredness, its similarity to evangelical Christian music. However, there are important elements of CJM that, in being rejected in the UK, help to reinforce problematic elements of the UK Jewish community.

CJM is based on the blurring of boundaries within the Jewish community. The blurring of the boundary between worship and performance is problematic within the British Jewish community as it challenges the idea of the synagogue as a place of worship separate from everyday life. CJM's ambiguity does not fit easily into a community that has fairly rigid ideas about how Jewish life should look. CJM, and Debbie Friedman in particular, also challenge notions about who can be a leader in the Jewish community. English-language songwriting, a lack of emphasis on musical virtuosity, and an emphasis on participation and song-leading – all of these aspects help to make CJM a reasonably democratic musical form. Furthermore, the example of Debbie Friedman shows that CJM can not only be very open to women's participation, but it can also empower women as leaders and contributors to liturgy. With its Orthodox majority, the British Jewish community is less open to female leadership and participation, and is founded on a much less democratic institutional structure.

Alternatives to CJM – ethnic and neo-Hassidic music

If CJM reveals the differences between the UK and British Jewish communities, other forms of Jewish music display a much closer relationship. In the past few decades there has been a considerable revival of 'ethnic' Jewish music; that is, music that is not so heavily tied to religious and liturgical contexts and meanings. The most important ethnic Jewish music to be revived is klezmer, the celebratory music of the pre-holocaust *shtetl*. The klezmer revival originated in America, when a new generation rediscovered their parents' and grandparents' music in the 1960s and 1970s. However, the klezmer revival has become a global movement (Slobin 2000) and is as significant in Europe as it is in America. To be sure, there are differences between klezmer in different locations – continental European klezmer is often played and enjoyed by non-Jews (Gruber 2002). However, klezmer and ethnic Jewish music does provide a much more equal 'bridge' between Europe and America than CJM does. British musicians such as Sophie Solomon have collaborated with American musicians and there is considerable multi-directional touring traffic.

In the sense that it requires a level of skill to play, klezmer is much more elitist than CJM. However, klezmer and ethnic Jewish music are a lot more open to participation by a wider range of Jews than CJM, and there are many secular, progressive Jews involved in it. Given that ethnic Jewish music is generally not focused on religious practice and meaning, it is potentially more open to be used in cross-communal settings than religious Jewish musics such as CJM. In the UK, where the community is strongly divided along religious lines, ethnic Jewish music can be a unifier. That much of the ethnic Jewish musical repertoire is instrumental helps in this as it removes the Orthodox 'problem' of women singing (though perhaps not the problem of mixed dancing).

Although all Jewish music is ultimately syncretic and borrowed, to contemporary, Western ears ethnic Jewish music somehow 'sounds' Jewish. As such, it is potentially of more interest than CJM to British Jews who are concerned that their Jewish involvement should feel somehow traditional and authentic. The same is true for the forms of neo-Hassidic music that have emerged since the 1960s. A crucial figure in this world is Rabbi Shlomo Carlebach (d. 1994), the 'singing rabbi'. Carlebach was an orthodox musician who became known in the 1960s for his fusion of 1960s folk music and Hassidic styles. A prolific composer, he contributed many melodies and *niggunim* (songs without words) to the Jewish canon. Carlebach attempted to proselytise amongst non-observant Jews and his music has a large following across the Jewish spectrum. This includes the Reform movement where, in recent years, Carlebach melodies have become popular within the liturgy (Summit 2000). This is the case in the UK as well as America. Whereas CJM has made few inroads into liturgical life in the UK, Carelbach-style neo-Hassidic music appears to be much more acceptable. While neo-Hassidic worship, like CJM, foregrounds spirituality in the Jewish experience, it does so via a musical medium that feels far more authentic to British Jews.

Conclusion: Jews united and divided through music

For Jews, questions of Jewish music can never simply be questions of taste. Music permeates Jewish practice, not simply within 'religious' contexts but in 'secular' ones as well. Whereas it is possible to simply avoid or dismiss other forms of music that one dislikes, any Jew with anything more than a nominal connection to the Jewish community encounters Jewish music. Not liking CJM, or any other Jewish music, has consequences for the Jewish community and ones own and others' Jewish identities. While taste is never neutral in any context whatever, its connection with identity and practice in the Jewish – and other religious – contexts is particularly strong.

It is inconceivable in a global community as large and as diverse as the Jewish community that there should be any unanimity as to what good Jewish music consists of and what is musically appropriate in a Jewish setting. The example of CJM, together with ethnic and neo-Hassidic music, demonstrate both this lack of unanimity and also the ability of Jewish music to create connections between and generate change within Jewish communities in different locations. Questions of Jewish music are inseparable from questions of Jewish identity and practice. CJM raises a range of complex issues such as the nature of liturgy, the position of spirituality in Jewish life and the nature of Jewish communal leadership. Musical controversies are both epiphenomenal to such questions and help to animate them in accessible ways.

The case study discussed in this chapter affirms the idea that there are substantial differences between American and European models of religion. It also shows that these differences should not be seen to mean that the systems are mutually exclusive. Rather, the Jewish world, like the Christian, Muslim, Hindu and other religious worlds, is permeated by forces of unification and fragmentation that work on a global scale. Music provides a valuable way of tracing the contours of these complicated global forces.

5

The Return of Ziryab

Yusuf Islam on Music

Göran Larsson

With the album *An Other Cup*, Yusuf Islam (formerly known as Cat Stevens), returned to the music industry. On his conversion to Islam in 1977, Cat Stevens, one of the brightest and most commercial pop stars of the 1970s, gave up his stardom, abandoned the music industry and changed his name to Yusuf Islam. Although his conversion to Islam was not conditioned, and he says openly that he felt no pressure to leave the music scene, Yusuf Islam turned his back on show business for almost two decades.[1] This decision was based on his conviction that the music industry had a destructive side and that it was not good for him. The choice to stop recording music and performing live was ultimately his own. With the release of *An Other Cup* in 2006 his opinion on music had clearly changed.

This chapter aims to cast light on how and why Yusuf Islam changed his mind about music. In order to discuss Yusuf Islam's opinions of music it is, however, first necessary to give a brief overview of the position of music in Islamic theology and history. This discussion of the historical and theological background is intended to serve as a backdrop to the case of Yusuf Islam, and so is far from comprehensive. It is essential to stress at the outset that it is not possible to find *one* unified so-called Islamic or Muslim opinion on music that is embraced by all Muslims. As with other questions, the Muslim community is divided in its opinions on the suitability or harmfulness of music.

Despite the fact that many Muslim theologians have been sceptical towards music, singing and dancing, historical records and ethnographic accounts clearly indicate that there has been, and still is, a gap between the religious elite and 'ordinary' Muslims. Even though some influential contemporary theologians (see below) condemn music as something sinful and forbidden, it is clear that many individuals with Muslim cultural backgrounds – especially among the youth born and raised in Europe and the United States, but also in the Middle East and Asia – are devoted listeners to, for example, raï-music from North Africa, *kawali* music from Pakistan, and so-called Western secular music (i.e. pop music, rock'n roll and even heavy metal) (see, for example, Gazzah 2008 and LeVine 2008). Music has always been part of the popular culture and it often plays important functions at weddings, funerals and festivals (Marcus 2007). And several music groups today label themselves as 'Muslim' or 'Islamic' groups, especially within the hip hop and rap genre. For these groups, music is either a method for calling people to Islam, or a way of letting off steam (i.e. protesting against discrimination, segregation, racism, or global politics).[2]

Islam and music

As already indicated, Muslim theologians have often expressed negative opinions about music, singing and dancing.[3] Despite the fact that music is not directly addressed in the Koran, a large number of so-called *hadith*-reports (i.e. records of the sayings and doings of the Prophet Muhammad) address music and related topics. On the one hand, the prophetic reports contain examples of the Prophet Muhammad forbidding certain forms of music and specific instruments (especially stringed instruments). But on the other hand, *hadith*-reports also transmit information that indicates that the Prophet Muhammad occasionally sang, or that he at least tolerated singing during hard work. Although it is hard to find one single explanation for the criticism, music is generally associated with pre-Islamic society. This society is stereotypically presented as a decadent and immoral community that contradicted the ideal Islamic society. Music is also presented as a force that can lead mankind astray and divert the individual from paying absolute attention to Allah. Music is associated with negative values and immoral behaviours such as drinking and dancing, which all 'true' Muslims should avoid if they want to remain faithful Muslims (Hjärpe 2001; Hammond 2005; Marcus 2007).

Notwithstanding the stark opposition towards music, the ritualised remembrance of God (in Arabic known as *dhikr*) is closely linked to various forms of musical expression, dancing, clapping hands and certain instruments (especially the reed flute *ney*). For example, during the *dhikr*-ritual performed by the Turkish Mevlavi order, better known as the whirling dervishes, music and dancing play a key role in the religious sermon as well as in the theology of the followers of this particular order (Marcus 2007: 43–59). During the *dhikr* the name of God or parts of the Islamic creed are repeated according to specific patterns, tempos and forms. This ritual, which can take different forms depending on local contexts and theological settings, is closely linked to music.

It is also difficult to make a sharp distinction between singing and the recitation of the Koran (known in Arabic as *tajwid*).[4] Although most, if not all, Muslim theologians stress that the recitation of the Koran should not be compared with singing, it is evident that the division between recitation and music is in the ear of the beholder. Still the theologians underline that there is a difference between music and recitation. For example, the person who recites the Koran must have the correct intention (*niyya*) and he or she must be ritually clean (having performed the minor *wudu* or the larger *ghusl*) before touching and reciting the Koran. Nevertheless, it is evident that the listeners could experience the recitation of the Koran as a kind of music. The difference between theory and reality is critically discussed by, for example, Kristina Nelson in her book *The Art of Reciting the Qur'an*. She writes:

> [L]istener response to a melodic recitation may not correlate with theoretical perception of it as a unique art, separate from music. This circumstance is most visible in listener behavior and media treatment of professional reciters. Several factors are responsible. First, the melodic recitation shares a number of aspects with music in addition to pitch organization, such as ornamentation, a body of descriptive terminology, emotional and physical responses, and aesthetic and economic standards. Second, although the ideal recitation may not be called music, a certain musicality, such as use of melody and

vocal artistry, is not only accepted but required to fulfill the intent of the ideal. This requirement is based on the recognition of the power of music in general to engage the emotions and thus involves the listener more totally in the recitation.[5]

The thin line between the recitation of the Koran and popular music has also been trodden by numerous Arab pop singers. The best-known example may be the Egyptian singer Umm Kulthum (d. 1973) – know as *al-Sitt* (the Lady) – who drove her audience into an emotional frenzy when she used her voice in accordance with classical patterns. The Arab audience could easily be compared to the teenagers becoming hysterical over Elvis or the Beatles in Europe and the United States in the 1950s and 1960s. Although it is difficult to demonstrate that she deliberately used her knowledge of *tajwid* in her music, it is evident that she had learned the art of reciting the Koran in her youth. According to, for example, Andrew Hammond she had a perfect 'pronunciation of Quranic Arabic' and she used her singing technique with great perfection from the rise of Gamal Abdel Nasser in the 1950s until her death in 1973 (Hammond 2005: 146).

With the growing influence of Western music in the Middle East and in other places were Muslims live (for example in Europe and the United States) the debate about music is far from over. Today it is easy to find theologians who prohibit all forms of music, but a growing number argue that it is the intention and the content of the music that matters (see, for example, Marcus 2007). An example of a more conservative outlook can be found in the writings of the Egyptian-born theologian Yusuf al-Qaradawi (b. 1926), who is one of the most cited and influential Muslim theologians in the contemporary Muslim debate.[6] Even he argues that it is the locality and conditions of the performance, and the intention of the singer and the listener that determine if the song or the music is lawful (*halal*) or forbidden (*haram*) (Al-Qaradawi 2001: 296–300). A similar way of putting the argument is also found in the writings of the Egyptian-Swiss theologian and philosopher Tariq Ramadan (b. 1962). He strives to make Islamic values accepted and compatible with so-called Western values. Through his exegesis he is trying to help the large Muslim minority living in Europe and the United States to become better integrated and accepted as equals in the contemporary Western world. In accordance with the opinion of Yusuf al-Qaradawi, discussed above, he argues that music and singing is lawful under the right conditions. They are:

1. The content of singing or the type of music must remain in agreement with Islamic ethics and not bring about an attitude which contradicts them.

2. Interpretation (its mode, moment and place) must also respect these ethics.

3. This kind of entertainment must not lead people to forget their obligation towards God and fellow humans.

4. It is appropriate for the musician and the one who listens to him to measure, in full conscience, the impact and place that this art really takes in their lives. It is a question of establishing a balance of conscience which cannot be but personal and individual. (Ramadan 1999: 203)

Ramadan's list seems to empower the individual. According to his exegesis, it is the individual who has to decide from case to case whether music is a problem or not. Thus, if the content of the music and the intention of the musician/singer is lawful (halal) and not contrary to the 'ethics of Islam', and the place of the performance is not harmful to Muslims, it is up to individuals to choose whether they want to listen to it or not. But if the music contains explicit lyrics (referring to sex, drugs and alcohol) or if it is performed in a context (for example in a bar or at a club) where alcohol is served, it is harmful for Muslims. Also 'good' or 'lawful' music can become a problem if it become more important for the individual than performing the obligatory Muslim rituals (for example the five prayers).

It is clear that Muslim theologians hold different opinions about the suitability of listening to music. While some theologians take a firm stance against all forms of music, others are more liberal and open to the fact that singing and music are part of being human. To distance oneself from this particular aspect of human life could even be seen as a way of limiting the omnipotence of God. Thus, it is relevant to ask if music can be a method for calling people to Islam. Instead of posing a problem for Muslims, music might be used for a good purpose if it is performed with the correct intention. With this backdrop in mind it is time to turn to Yusuf Islam and his opinions on music and Islam.

Yusuf Islam on music

At the time of the release of the album *An Other Cup*, Yusuf Islam explained in an interview with *The Guardian*'s Alexis Petridis that he was never forced to leave the music industry. When he embraced Islam, he was even encouraged by the imam of the Central Mosque in London to continue with his music and carry on recording songs of a high moral standard with non-offensive lyrics. However, contrary to this advice, he came to the conclusion that it was best for him to put an end to his music career. Yusuf Islam explains: 'I heard another voice saying this is a dangerous business, you should be away from it, all the associations that go along with that way of life, you should get away from' (Petridis 2006).

Following this voice, Yusuf Islam came to the conclusion that it was best to take the 'safest position and get out'.[7] Back in 1976–77, he (i.e. Cat Stevens) was tired of the music industry, especially its commercialism, materialism and the ego boost of being a superstar.[8] Before his conversion to Islam he had been looking for alternative ways of life and he had tried to find happiness and peace in other religions (especially in Buddhism). However, in 1976 he was given a copy of the Koran by his brother and it was this gift that opened the gateway to Islam. To Stevens the Koran encompassed the truth he had been seeking for a long time.[9]

Despite his decision to put an end to his music career in 1977 he never promised that this break was final, or that it should last forever. In an interview in 1980 Yusuf Islam explained that he had abandoned his music career because he feared that it might divert him from the 'true path' of God. But he added: 'I will not be dogmatic in saying that I will never make music again. You can't say that without adding Insha Allah.'[10]

Because of the many letters Yusuf Islam received from people around the world who told him that his lyrics and songs had had a positive influence on their lives he began to change his mind about music. Some of his fans told him that he had saved their lives and stopped people from committing suicide. By listening to his music they had found a new, positive meaning in life.[11] After his conversion to Islam these positive letters took on a whole new meaning for Yusuf Islam. To save one human life is to save the whole of humanity, according to a famous tradition of the Prophet Muhammad (i.e. a *hadith*-report). But the single most important incident that made him change his opinion on music was the Balkan conflict in the early 1990s. He says:

> Since the genocide against Bosnia in 1992, I learned how important motivational songs are in keeping people's spirits high during times of great calamity. One of the things that changed me greatly was listening to the cassettes coming out of the Balkans at that time; these were rich and highly motivating songs (*nasheeds*), inspiring the Bosnians with the religious spirit of faith and sacrifice. (Yusuf Islam 2007)

As explained above, music is a controversial and debated issue within Islamic traditions and among Muslim theologians. Yusuf Islam is well aware of this tension, but he emphasises that music is a part of Islamic and Muslim history and Muslims should therefore not neglect or forget its impact on their culture and history. Even the Prophet Muhammad accepted and approved of certain kinds of music. Like most contemporary theologians, Yusuf Islam does however stress that this historical fact should not be seen as an indication that all forms of music are acceptable and in line with the spirit of Islam. He concludes:

> We must distinguish: for example, what is the message in the words of the song? What is the moral context and environment where the songs are being played? What is the time it is happening? Who is delivering the song? How is it delivered? And importantly, what is the intention? Some scholars say that as long as it conforms to moral norms and doesn't divert a person from his or her duties in worshipping Allah Most High, then it has its place in the culture of Islam. (Yusuf Islam 2007)

In another dialogue, Yusuf Islam made a similar point:

> Music can be a tool for social good as well as education and spiritual upliftment; it can also be corruptive and

time-wasting, so we must always be on guard not to fall into those traps. (Yusuf Islam 2003)

This way of approaching the question of Islam and music made Yusuf Islam change his mind about being involved in the music industry. In the 1990s he performed at various charity concerts for victims of AIDS, and in 2005 he organised a concert to help the victims of the tsunami catastrophe in East Asia at Christmas 2004. Some of these performances were also recorded to raise money for relief and to help victims of natural disasters and disease.[12] In October 2003, Yusuf Islam organised a concert – 'The Night of Remembrance' – in the Royal Albert Hall to celebrate the 20th anniversary of the establishment of his independent Islamic school, the Islamia Primary School in London.[13] The title of the concert (Night of Remembrance) is a clear reference to the Arabic concept *Laylat al-Qadr* ('The Night of Power)'. According to Islamic theology this night is believed to be the anniversary of the night when the Koran was first revealed to the Prophet Muhammad. It is also believed that requests made to God during this night will be granted. Zain Bhikha, Native Deen and Khalid Belrhouz and other Muslim artists supported and joined Yusuf Islam in this concert, and Abdal-Hakim Murad and Hamza Yosuf, two well-known Muslim theologians, gave speeches at the concert to clarify the Islamic standpoint on peace and remembrance.[14] During the 1990s, Yusuf Islam also recorded two albums with Islamic educational songs for children and two edifying records for Muslim adults.[15]

Today it is clear that Yusuf Islam has changed his opinion about music. For instance, at the 2006 Nobel Peace Prize Concert banquet he performed together with a number of commercial non-Muslim artists (for instance Lionel Richie and Simply Red). The artists at the Nobel Concert honoured, for example, Muhammad Yunus of Bangladesh and the Grameen Bank. The aim of Yunus's project was help people rise above poverty by giving them small loans to start businesses. At this concert Yusuf Islam performed 'Peace Train' and 'Moon Shadow', two of his most beloved and classic songs from the Cat Stevens era. In a press statement before the concert he explained that he had many reasons for playing music today. He said: 'Today there are perhaps 101 good reasons why I feel right making music and singing about life in this fragile world again.'[16] For example, before singing 'Peace train', Yusuf

Islam explained that poverty is a major obstacle to peace and that he was happy to sing this particular song for the Nobel Peace Prize winner Muhammad Yunus, who won the prize because of his fight against poverty.[17] However, it is also likely that Yusuf Islam has changed his opinion about the lyrics. For instance, 'Peace train' can easily be interpreted as a song that carries some of the basic values of Islam. Like the lyrics in this song, Islam is generally understood as a message of goodness for mankind that speaks of unity and peace in the world. The necessity of helping the world to become a better place is central in Islamic theology and the line of the song that reads 'Oh peace train take this country, come take me home again' can without great difficulties be understood as a reference to the kingdom of God.

Still it is clear that Yusuf Islam travelled a long road between his commercial record *Back to Earth* in 1977 and his latest album *An Other Cup*. In a so-called Live Dialogue session on the Internet organised by IslamOnline.net in December 2003, Yusuf Islam explained that there is a 'wide difference between a sex-driven disco and morally motivating devotional songs'. In the same answer he says that he has tried his best to make music that is in line with his understanding of Islam and therefore 'I personally do not use guitars or other musical instruments other than percussion'.[18] The conclusion that certain instruments are unacceptable is found among many Muslim theologians, but at the Nobel Peace Prize concert Yusuf Islam played the guitar. In an interview for the same website in 2006, he explains his views on this topic:

> When my son brought the guitar back into the house you know, that was the turning point. It opened a flood of, of new ideas and music which I think a lot of people would connect with.[19]

This quote shows how Yusuf Islam's opinion on music has matured since his break with the music industry back in 1977. Today he emphasises that it is essential for mankind to bridge the gap between the material and spiritual world, and to do this it is important to revitalise some of the positive feelings of the 1970s. Unity, kindness, peace and positivity are concepts that are close to both the hippie era and the basic values of Islam and other religions.[20]

Muslim opinions on Yusuf Islam's return to music

When Cat Stevens left the music industry and declared that he had embraced Islam, many fans were disappointed, and the press was filled with negative stories and false rumours. The situation became even worse when Stevens refused to give interviews and explain his decision. He was also portrayed as a supporter of the revolution in Iran in 1979 and later of Ayatollah Khomeini's fatwa against Salman Rushdie and the publication of the book *The Satanic Verses*.[21] Even though he had no knowledge of or responsibility for the revolution in Iran, he was often held accountable in the British press. According to Yusuf Islam, this was a difficult period and he often felt uneasy with the whole situation. The press was asking difficult questions and he was portrayed as a figurehead even though he had little or no knowledge about Middle Eastern politics or Islam for that matter. Before he could go public, he had to learn more about Islam and become comfortable with the new situation.

If the reactions in Europe and the United States were dominated by shock, disappointment and even anger, his conversion was hardly noticed by Muslims in the Middle East, Europe or the United States. When he said yes to Islam and declared the *shahada* (the Islamic creed – 'There is no God but God and Muhammad is the messenger of God') in the Central Mosque in London, few Muslims noticed that it was the megastar Cat Stevens who had become a Muslim.[22] If his conversion had little impact, how did Muslims react to his decision to take up music again and release a brand new album? Before outlining some of the reactions that I have come across it is important to stress that it is hardly possible to find a unified Islamic opinion on any issue – Muslims are of course divided along theological, geographical, economic, social and political lines and it is not possible to speak of a monolithic Muslim culture. My analysis of the reactions that followed the release of *An Other Cup* in 2006 is limited to the influential and widely quoted Sunni Muslim website IslamOnline.net which is based in Egypt and Qatar.[23] Although it is difficult to argue that this website gives voice to a specific interpretation of Islam, most of the information and theological exegesis presented on the site belongs to a so-called *salafi*, or reformist/modernist interpretation of Islam. Several of those who publish on this site are also more or less influenced by the ideology and theology of the Muslim Brotherhood movement, a reformist or Islamist movement with roots in Egypt. The key figure of the website is Yusuf al-Qaradawi, mentioned above. In the same way as the founding fathers of the reformist movement in the late nineteenth and early twentieth centuries, most messages posted on IslamOnline.net try to find an interpretation of Islam that is in harmony with modernity without giving up an Islamic identity. The aim is to find a middle way between extremism and secularism in order to make it possible to be a 'faithful' Muslim in a modern society.

It should therefore come as no surprise that the return of Yusuf Islam to the music industry has been noted in several messages and articles on the homepage of IslamOnline.net. In general, most voices have been positive and supportive. According to Meymuna Hussain, Yusuf Islam is blessed with a unique talent to touch the lives of many peoples, Muslims and non-Muslims alike, and with this talent comes great responsibility. From a Muslim point of view, he has a great ability to do *da'wa* (to call people to Islam). Hence, he should use his gift to present the Muslim way of life in an attractive and understandable way so non-Muslims can understand the greatness of Islam (Hussain 2001; cf. Janson 2002). Hussain enthuses:

> His message transcends nationalistic and spiritual barriers, allowing him to speak to the hearts and minds of anyone, anywhere, at all times, and all places . . . including this young Muslimah on the 605 freeway. (Hussain 2001)

Other messages on the IslamOnline.net website also highlight that Yusuf Islam has taken a clear stance for peace. Several of his early songs (especially 'Peace Train' from the album *Teaser and the Firecat* that was released in 1971) are positive examples for all mankind. His backing of the Islamia School in the UK and his support of the relief organisation Small Kindness are also emphasised on the site.[24] The release of *An Other Cup* was highlighted in two articles and there is to the best of my knowledge no criticism of his decision to return to the music; that is, as long as the music is in harmony with basic Islamic opinions.[25]

It seems as if Yusuf Islam has come to terms with the fact that he is a talented singer-songwriter and that he can use his stardom, fame and charisma to call people to Islam and to raise money for charity.

But his conversion to Islam can also serve as a positive example and a counterweight to the overwhelming negative media coverage of Islam and Muslims in the West. From this point of view, he illustrates that well-educated, talented and peaceful Westerners also can embrace Islam without become fanatics or radicals (see, for example, Allievi 2002).

The return of Ziryab: A way of conclusion

When interviewed for the *Guardian*, Yusuf Islam showed the journalist Alexis Petridis a deluxe edition of *An Other Cup* that contains a picture of 'himself drinking coffee underneath a poster that reads *The return of Ziryab*'. This reference is interesting in that Abu 'L-Hasan 'Ali b. Nafi' Ziryab is an historical person who is portrayed as a multi-talented musician, intellectual, textile designer, astronomer and gastronome in Muslim historiography. Ziryab was probably born around the year 790 and he served under the Caliph al-Mahdi in Baghdad, but due to political turbulence he had to move to North Africa. In 822 he arrived at Córdoba and served the Andalusian Caliph Abd al-Rahman II until his death in 852.[26] Like Ziryab, Yusuf Islam could be described as a person who functions as a bridge between the oriental and occidental cultures. Ziryab is described as a person who tried to renew the cultural language (especially by introducing new musical genres and styles), and in this way he closed the gap between different cultures. Regardless of whether this description is true or not, Ziryab is held in high esteem by Muslims and it is not hard to see why Yusuf Islam is fascinated with him. From the interviews and articles published by Yusuf Islam it is clear that he also wants to be perceived and remembered as an artist who built bridges between the Muslims and non-Muslims. It is therefore his mission to improve the image of Islam and show a non-Muslim audience that Islam can bring peace of mind, happiness and something positive to the world. This mission is clearly manifest in the following quotation taken from the *Guardian* interview.

> Maybe some people may have thought or imagined that Islam drains all creativity. For me, to sing again means to reaffirm the creativity of Islam though, of what it can do to a person and how it can express itself. (Petridis 2006)

In conclusion, the return of Yusuf Islam to the music industry carries both a political and religious dimension and it is his mission is to show that Islam is not a religion that promotes terrorists or extremism. On the contrary, he argues, Islam can function as a positive force in a destructive and negative world that fosters nothing but suspicion and hostility between Muslims and non-Muslims. From this point of view, Yusuf Islam could be seen as a *da'i*, i.e. a person who calls mankind to God and who preaches Islam.[27] Consequently, his mission resembles that of Abu 'L-Hasan 'Ali b. Nafi Ziryab who was eager to bring together the oriental and occidental worlds by breaching the divisions between them. His aim was to bridge the imagined gap between Muslims and non-Muslims and enrich human culture. To put it in the words of Cat Stevens, now is the time to jump on the peace train and change the world into a better place for all mankind.

6

The Meanings of the Religious Talk in French Rap Music

Stéphanie Molinero

Rapping is a cultural, artistic and social expression born in the African American ghettos of New York. It found in France a perfect place to develop, and French rap has been active for more than 25 years. In fact, today France is considered by many observers to be the 'second nation' of rap.[1]

Rap was originally introduced to France by a small number of artists who created what is known today as 'the old school', but its development on French soil was furthered by a new generation of artists, those of 'the new school', who were responsible for new directions and the 'complexification' of French rap.

The aim here is to explain the evolution of French rap and the current issues with which it is confronted, of which religion is one. Indeed, the religious aspect seems to be a significant direction in the evolution of the new French rap scene. This chapter, based on a thesis concerning the problem of what is called 'popular'[2] in the analysis of existing music and especially current French rap, offers reflections about the introduction and development of the theme of religion in French rap music.

Twenty-five years of the French rap scene

Until the mid-1990s, the French rap scene was mainly dominated by a few artists. While the 'underground' rap scene included many artists, only a few reached national recognition beyond the underground audience. MC Solaar, IAM, NTM and the group Assassin are some of these artists. MC Solaar's cool, melodious and poetical rap contrasts with the social and political style of NTM, Assassin or even IAM. The term 'hardcore' is used to designate the most virulent tendency of this social and political rap, of which NTM's two members have been the most outstanding figures for many years.

Hugues Bazin asserts, however, that that the distinction between 'cool rap' and 'hardcore rap' that has been made since the mid-1990s is a very artificial one that only partially represents the complexity of the different tendencies in French rap music.[3] The division between 'cool' and 'hardcore' rap, even if it can easily be understood from a musical point of view, breaks down if we refer to the message content. According to Bazin (1995), 'cool rap' also protests; its content is the same as 'hardcore rap'. The only thing that makes it different from hardcore is its musical content, which is more mannered. Similarly, the rap called 'hardcore', even if it denounces/exposes some social problems, also creates 'an esthetic quality of thought, [. . .] a new urban poetry'.

Even if the analysis of the musical content actually enables us to distinguish two different global musical processes, the social content is present both in 'cool' rap and 'hardcore' rap. Hence this distinction is partly artificial, and does not really attest to the original unity of the talk developed by French rap.

A decade or so after Hugues Bazin's words, it had become more difficult to view French rap as a unified whole because of the development of so many new movements. From a strictly musical point of view (i.e. referring only to the musical accompaniment, not the lyrics), it used to be easier to distinguish the 'cool' productions, which were more melodious and harmonious, from the 'hardcore' productions, which were jerkier, more staccato and rhythmical. But recent developments, and especially the slowing down of the beat, today make the distinction more difficult to see. Still from a musical point of view, the main differences that are distinguishable today in French productions are the artists' general musical influences.

If some of them continue to refer to African American music (mainly jazz, soul, and funk), some other productions draw their inspiration from other musical styles such as rock and roll (indeed even punk rock), electronic or even world music.

Moreover, if Hugues Bazin considered in 1995 that rap music's global message (whether it it was 'hardcore' or 'cool') was the same for all rappers, today it is very difficult to make general statements about French rap's textual productions. Some of them, descendants of the first generation of French rap, are still making demands and protesting with a strong social and political message, but many new tendencies have arisen.

Referring specifically to the thematic content of French rap's productions, it is possible to distinguish different general tendencies: a social and political rap (personified, for example, by the band La Rumeur[4]) but also what can be called 'street-rap' (*rap de rue*) including, for example, the productions of the rappers Booba and Rohff, who focus on the reality of French suburban ghettos[5] (describing them without any other social or political talk); a rap that the hip hop adherents call 'bling-bling' (partly inspired by American rap, dealing with comfort and material enjoyment), or even a more introspective rap such as Oxmo Puccino's productions which speaks less about the rapper's personality as a 'ghetto' representative and more about his sensibility as a human being.

Some other distinctions are present within the French rap scene: those which concern the text's treatment, for example. Indeed, the aim of some rappers is to describe social reality in its more brutal aspect, whereas others will try to focus on the text itself, working on the vocabulary, the metaphors they use, the style of their rhymes, etc. The different means of distribution also become factors of the current rap scene's differentiation; while 'underground' productions rarely attract the attention of the mass media, the rap produced by a few artists contracted to record labels enjoys wider distribution, especially through the musical radio channel Skyrock, which currently is the only nationwide channel specialising in rap. There is a clear split between radio rap and that which remains underground. In the case of underground rap, media coverage and distribution are only possible through the underground network (specialised shops, magazines, street marketing), or through the Internet.

The process of diversification of rap productions and their means of distribution is mirrored by diversification in the consumers of this music in France. There are two generations within the rap audience: the older ones remain attached to the early French rap productions, while the second generation of rap receivers generally prefers more recent artists. The sense of belonging to a generation is actually the first sign of differentiation within the rap audience. But there is also a social differentiation: according to their social origin and their membership in a certain class, rap fans will prefer some artists over others.

There appears to be greater diversity among both artists and audiences in this new rap generation compared with the first generation of French rap. Current French rap productions still sound quite different from other French musical productions, because of the use of French rap's own verbal scansion. This apparent unity masks the multiplicity of current trends in rap, and because of this it is difficult to point out any other unifying elements in the French rap scene.

In this connection, analysis of the religion theme could be very interesting. Trying to understand the change from French old school to French new school through this thematic, we can distinguish two similarities between rap and religion. First, rap's oral scansion is very similar to that of a sermon, and second, the use of sampling shows that rap resembles the religious sermon (which also gathers samples from the entirety of the writings of the preacher's religious denomination) (Lapassade and Rousselot 1991).

Yet, these formal elements, which bring rap and religious talk together, have not always led to the expression of a religious discourse (a discourse deriving its references and themes from a religion). To understand how French rap talk and religious speech can be seen as similar to each other, it is necessary to understand how French rap was linked to religion from the start.

The emergence of hip hop in France and the appearance of a 'hip hop religiosity'

In early French rap, the religious question can only be clearly discerned if we consider the dichotomy between the sacred and the profane which defines every religion. According to Hugues Bazin, who made a study of the burgeoning French hip hop movement, the whole variety of hip hop expressions (rap, graffiti, tags, break-dance and deejaying) 'limits "another world" revealing sacred places'. So the French hip hop movement, like every religion, is built on the principle of distinction between initiates and the profane. Nevertheless, the separation between the profane and initiates is not materialised in hip hop. Its activities, at least at the beginning of the movement, took place in the street, which is a profane place, unlike the institutionalised religions which have their own places of worship. The frontier between sacred and profane must be understood here as a 'mental frontier which separates initiates from ignorant people, those who evolve in a parallel system (the hip hop one) and the others, all the others' (Vicherat 2001).

Even if a new form of religion appears very early for French hip hop performers and fans and even if some of them already had some kind of relationship with God, hip hop is considered a 'religiosity without any religion', 'no matter one's own religion' (Bazin 1995).

Just as French hip hop adherents are characterised by their ethnic diversity being unified through hip hop in 'an intervening state of mind creating a cultural space as such' (Bazin 1995), the different hip hop adherents' religions (mainly Catholic and Muslim) are also joined together through hip hop and its values.

Rapper Kool Shen, from the band NTM, explains some of these values, recalling in a song recorded in 1995 the first steps of hip hop in France:

> Naïve, inexperienced but very proud of evolving in a parallel system, where the basic values were a jumble of *Peace, Unity, Love and Having Fun*, Hip Hop never needed guns or gangs, toys or bands, but only more faith from those who defend memory and the code of ethics which are the essential values.[6]

The term 'parallel system' refers to the distinction between those who belong to the movement and the outsiders. The use of the term 'faith' also refers to a certain sense of belonging and beliefs related to hip hop which is here understood as a religion according to the primary sense of the Latin term *religare* (to link up, to connect).

Hip hop values in France come from the message of the Zulu Nation, even though this movement did not succeed in establishing itself on a long-term and organised basis in France.

The Zulu Nation was founded in the United States in the mid-1970s by the rapper Afrika Bambaataa. His aim was to capture the negative energy of young people living in the American ghettos (blacks and Puerto Ricans, but also all the youths of the world living in such situations) and turn it into a constructive force through the street culture, hip hop. The Zulu Nation bases its message on themes such as: no more races, no more violence, no more drugs, no more hate. It provides rules for behaving according to its values, and its members must be in search of peace, non-violence, wisdom and self-knowledge.

The Zulu Nation's collective dimension appears through its goal of unifying its members. This idea is also part of the slogan: 'Love, peace and unity.' The Zulu Nation thereby provided common values to the hip hop movement, first in the USA and then abroad.

The Zulu Nation established itself in France in the 1980s, but the movement did not really take firm root at the time.

First, the French Zulu Nation had difficulties not only in finding an identity, but also in being recognised and in differentiating itself from the 'young ghetto gangs' also called 'Zulus' by the tabloids (Boucher 1998). By condemning tags and the use of soft drugs,

> it failed to appear as a structure open to all those with some interest in Hip Hop. It was seen as a more severe, austere and uncompromising structure. It appeared to be disconnected from the needs and reality of young people interested in Hip Hop expression . . . Even if some rappers were receptive to the Zulu Nation's message, most of them saw it as a quite old institution, which was a little bit 'moralist' and above all elitist . . . [indeed,] only a small number of chosen ones, selected according to well-defined criteria, could aspire to belong to the Zulu Nation. So the Zulu Nation is still an unreachable myth for most of them. (Boucher 1998)

The Zulu Nation did not succeed in finding its own model in France. According to Hugues Bazin, the movement's failure in France can be explained by the communitarian inspiration of the American model which is strongly imbued with Black consciousness and Africanism, and therefore 'hardly applicable in France'. However, thanks to the most globally spread part of its message, 'it is greatly to her credit that the French Zulu Nation gave a soul to the French Hip Hop movement' (Boucher 1998).

This soul, this state of mind, is carried by universal values such as non-violence and the fight against racism. That was the goal of the Zulu Nation. This 'soul' is also represented by many positive things: the challenge is a non-violent artistic competition where the individual tries to give his best. The self-respect and respect towards others are both values and attitudes promoted by the movement. The 'fresh' spirit objectivises itself in a cool, tolerant, pleasant attitude, and authenticity is shown to be a value which enables one to remain faithful to the hip hop state of mind. The words 'authentic' and 'authenticity' are often used by hip hop adherents. They represent both a practice and an attitude. The authentic person is the one who remains faithful to the state of mind which created hip hop, but also the one who, in his or her activities (no matter if he/she succeeds or not), considers the attachment to street-arts as essential.

In this way, the Zulu Nation's universal message, transposed to the French social context, enabled the hip hop movement to base itself on values and attitudes which, in their form and foundation, have certain similarities to religious talk. Yet, during the emergence of French hip hop (1980–95), the religious talk does not appear in rap, even if therer are indirect signs of spirituality and mysticism in some of the lyrics, such as those of the band IAM.[7]

The development of religious talk in French rap music

Researchers taking an interest in the religious question in French rap have mentioned no direct references to religion in rap lyrics before the year 1996. This does not mean that this type of talk did not exist prior to that; it was simply confined to the underground network.[8]

In 1995 Akhenaton, one of the members of IAM, whose Sicilian origins did not predispose him to adopt Islam, explained the reasons for his conversion to Islam: 'My evolution to Islam is a natural movement towards the most mystic and open religion . . . For me, the social aspect is the most important; political Islam has no significance for me.'[9]

Even if the reference to the Muslim religion is here still understood as a search for spirituality and mysticism, the conversion to Islam of this rapper – who belongs to one of the rap scene's main bands – announced the widening of the religious talk within French rap productions. From 1996, references to God or to a specific religion became more numerous in French rap. The New African Poets, also known as NAP, whose members originate from Africa, built up their collective identity by gathering around Islam. Islam appears then in their productions, especially in their song 'La mystique d'Adb al Malik'[10] in which their talk can be considered a form of 'proselytisation' (Vicherat 1998):

> It's not God who doesn't exist, it's the human being
> who simply can't see him.
> Our eyes are blinded by matter
> Limited by space
> But also time.
> God can only be seen through the eyes of our heart.
> The one who knows his soul, knows his Lord.[11]

Other artists also punctuate their works with references to Islam or more generally to God. Example are the Fonky Family,[12] Monsieur R,[13] Afrojazz,[14] or the rappers' collective La Boussole, whose name is a reference to the niche in the mosques indicating the direction of Mecca. Moreover, this rappers' collective is under contract to a record company called Din Records (*din* means religion in Arabic).

The reference to Muslim religion is also manifested in the streetwear market through the brand Billal Wear, which was created in 2000 and whose name refers to one of the first black men who converted to Islam.

The example of Kery James helps illuminate the evolution of religious talk within rap. Kery James is a rapper from the south Parisian suburbs. He started his career as the leader of the band Idéal J., and is well known for the harshness of his lyrics and for being deeply rooted in the reality of the French 'ghetto'. Violence, delinquency and crime are themes that figure prominently in the lyrics of his band, especially in their song 'Pour une poignée de dollars':[15]

> For a handful of dollars
> I would be killed for a handful of dollars . . .
> What would you do for a handful of dollars?

Maybe it will be too late
When you will know it, you damn fool!
Do you think that misery down here in this world is an illusion?
And that we like to visit our people in the visiting room?
Listen, look, for a handful of dollars
The ghetto youths are ready to go to jail
Deals, business, robberies in this period of crisis
You fool, accuse the power![16]

Many years later, on his album *Si c'était à refaire* ('If I could do it again from the start'), Kery James tells that he is a street survivor, but also that for many years he lived as both a rapper and a criminal and that he nearly went to prison several times.

After the death of one of his friends, which according to his texts was due to a gangland killing, and before recording this album, James became a Muslim, by which he recovered his pride (James 2001) and found new meaning and values in life.

In this album, which was realised without Idéal J.'s other members, James, who wants to expiate his past sins, emphasises in his talk the values of sharing, solidarity, peace and love with the goal of laying the foundation of a 'conscious' rap. This also provides an opportunity for him to explain how his conversion to Islam enabled him to change his opinion about the world:

I relearned to live
I've understood the causes of our decline
And when I look at my past, I've almost had it
If I didn't have Islam,
Maybe I would have been killed
Or would have spent half my life in prison.[17]

Since then, for James, religion has become an unshakable response to the divisions of inter- and intra-generation social cohesion among the disadvantaged in France, a bastion against the trap of crime, and a weapon against 'evil'.

In 2004, James continued to spread a message of fraternity, full of Muslim religiosity. Of the 21 tracks on his album *Savoir et vivre ensemble*,[18] six are religious chants interpreted by the APBIF (an Islamic charity in France). The profits from the sale of this album were donated to the association Savoir et Tolérance (Wisdom and Tolerance) in order to build a Muslim cultural centre, and also to a lay association.

Although Islam is the key of the project *Savoir et vivre ensemble*, Kery James invited rappers with different origins and religions to feature on the album 'in order to bring a different viewpoint on this religion through its universal values that every sensible person recognises as good: values such as respect, charity, generosity and humility' (rfimusique 2004). James created this project in order to help people to discover Islam and share its most universal values.

Moreover, the rapper declared in an interview that this album was a response to the media image of Islam: 'It's an album to fight against the way the media have been treating Islam since 11 September 2001' (ibid.). According to the artist, regardless of his own faith, a double process materialises in this album production. There is a desire to unite all the French hip hop artists, and also the audience, in values that are both Muslim and universal. It is also a reaction to the negative image of Islam. So this process is internal to the world of French hip hop, but it is also directed to the whole of French society.

Kery James's path, as well as the signs of an increase in religious talk in French rap productions, seem to reveal a deeper shift within the French rap scene; indeed, even within French society as a whole. In order to clearly analyse the place, functions, causes and the eventual consequences of explicit religious talk in French rap, we did a textual analysis of many current French rap productions. In 2003/04 rap listeners were surveyed to find out the names of their favourite rap artists, and the latest productions of these artists were analysed (a total of 12).

Religious speech in current French rap music

Of the 12 musical and textual productions analysed, seven deal with the question of religion. When this question is contemplated from an outside point of view, without any reference to the rapper's belief, the religion issue is tackled such a way as to denounce the manipulations of religions. In the opinion of the group Assassin, the French State has deliberately chosen not to integrate immigrant populations so that they will 'find refuge in prayer' and not worry about their being socially dominated. The group Sniper, on the other hand, puts forward the idea of the employment of religions by leaders of nations to commit people to the values of capitalism: 'It won't take long till they tell kids that dough is God.'[19] As for rapper Rohff, he draws attention to the lack of mutual understanding and communication between different religions.

Here, religion is treated as a set of themes, a leading angle through which the rapper reveals his own vision of the world; however he does not reveal his personal conception of religion. References to a personal view of religion appear in six of the textual productions analysed. This means that the theme of religious belief is not dominant within French rap music. It is nevertheless not a marginal phenomenon, either.

The six groups and artists who refer to religion on a personal level in their productions (Sniper, Rohff, 113, Kery James, Fonky Family and Booba) name God in a general way, and not as a character associated with any particular religion.

In any case, whenever a religious allusion can be noted, it is about Islam, referring either to its practices (Ramadan, the Eid feast, halal food), the Muslim God, Allah, or the holy book, the Koran. Kery James alone insists on the values passed on by Islam, which according to him appeal to human intelligence, knowledge, indulgence and patience. He also emphasises the positive effects this religion has on the human soul and the coherence of the social group: 'Islam brings love back.'[20]

Here is the first function assigned to religion: it unites men by putting universal and humanistic values at the centre of their preoccupations, as mentioned above.

The other rappers who explicitly refer to religion (whether Muslim or not) explain their personal relationships to religion without depicting the possible effects on a social group, whatever this group may be. In the best case, rappers appeal to God to support a single person: 'May God protect you',[21] (113), or returning to Kery James: 'May Allah preserve you from punishment.'[22]

Religious belief allows these rappers to transcend reality: 'great God'[23] (113), 'God is the greatest'[24] (Sniper) and to see the paths they pursued as God's decision: 'It was written it is no coincidence'[25] (Sniper), as well as for their future: 'Only what God prescribed can happen to me'[26] (Sniper), or else: 'One says fate is inevitable'[27] (Fonky Family).

On several occasions God is thanked, notably for having guided them towards rap music which is, for Sniper, a 'gift from God',[28] or, more generally, for allowing them to lead a more peaceful life through rap music: 'I thank God for having taken me out of my misery'[29] (Fonky Family), or for – someday – giving them success: 'I pray for providence'[30] (Rohff). But God is also feared; rappers reveal their submission to God as well as their fear of the Last Judgement: 'I hope that God and my family will forgive me'[31] (113), 'There's only One to whom you must explain yourself'[32] (113), 'Only God will judge me'[33] (Booba), or 'no one knows whether we'll go to Heaven or Hell'[34] (Fonky Family), whereas rapper Rohff appeals to God's mercy.

In a more pragmatic way, the rappers' relationships to God and religion enable them to overcome obstacles in life: 'Thanks to God, I overcome the obstacles'[35] (Rohff), 'If things aren't going fine, leave it to God'[36] (Fonky Family), and to go beyond one's violent and negative feelings: 'I answer my hatred telling myself God is grand'[37] (113). Faith prevents rappers from getting out of their depth, from sinking into mental distress: 'Faith as an antidepressant'[38] (Rohff), or into some traps of social life, into evil, often embodied as *chaytan* (an Arabic word meaning 'the devil'): 'into evil's darkness, I don't want to sink'[39] (Kery James), 'the Devil charms us'[40] (Sniper), even though the Fonky Family rappers confess they are caught 'in the cross-fire', between Good and Evil.

Whatever the rappers' representation of themselves may be, whether they are on the right or the wrong track, religious belief remains a guide in everyday life: 'my faith keeps me wide-awake'[41] (Rohff), 'May God guide me, I don't want to be wrong'[42] (Sniper).

Three of the six rappers insist that, 'despite everything', they keep the faith (Sniper, Fonky Family, Rohff), even if, in the case the group 113, faith is not that easy to keep alive. As one of the members of the group puts it, comparing his own faith to that of his father: 'I would like to be as much of a believer as my father.'[43]

Except for Kery James, who lauds the positive social effects that religious belief can achieve within a society, the rappers reveal their relationship to God in an individualistic fashion, without emphasising the functions of integration or social cohesion that religious belief can have. Religion acts as their support in everyday life; it helps them to differentiate good from evil (function of spiritual guide), supports them in moments of 'hatred' (function of channelling violence) or in moments which are morally difficult to overcome (function of emotional support) while revealing their personal imperfections (function of expiation) and their fear of divine judgement (function of domination, of submission).

How can we understand, in the specific framework of French rap music, how religion ensures these different functions? What is the reason for the relatively strong presence of religion – and notably Islam – in the lyrics of French rap?

Understanding the establishment of religious speech in French rap music

While rap and religion have been entangled in an intense relationship since the emergence of rap and hip hop in France, the religious line as such only appeared relatively recently in the lyrics of French rap.

In addition, rappers who adopt a religious line do not limit themselves to the underground sphere; their works are widely available (the artists whose texts are discussed above are all under contract with a major record label,[44] at least regarding the distribution of their CDs), and the also receive some attention from the mass media (in the form of Skyrock radio, in particular). Moreover, they enjoy a very favourable reception among a segment of the French population who are rap fans. What can be the explanation for the emergence of such a religious phenomenon?

As previously underlined, Kery James recorded his CD *Knowing and Living Together*[45] in reaction to the negative image of Islam conveyed by the media since 9/11.

However, in his lyrics, as well as in the lyrics of the other rappers we have examined, the international context is not directly linked with religious belief. Globally speaking, the rappers considered here all point to media disinformation, though they do not connect this idea to their denominational belonging or to their faith in God. The exception is the group Sniper, which recurrently tackles the international political context. It is within the framework of their treatment of the Israeli–Palestinian conflict that an indirect link can be drawn between the international context and the assertion of their religious belonging. In the song called 'Stone thrower' ('Jeteur de pierres'), which refers to the Intifada, Sniper seems to side with Palestinians; the song starts as follows:

> Establishing themselves in a land
> Becoming a resident, taking it over
> Expelling its inhabitants, miserable people
> Made to submit by a right of conquest and set
> Under the conqueror's political dependency
> Domineering quest
> Looking for a State
> Here is the result
> Of a colonising power
> Helped by the Occident.[46]

The group, while declaring that extremists exist in 'both camps' and that their wish is peace between the peoples, underlines the pro-Israeli position of the Western media and partly understands terrorism, whether Israeli or Palestinian. They also identify more with Palestinians than Israelis:

> What would you do if your father, your roof had been destroyed?
> I speak for myself: ouak' Allah
> I'd feel like causing absolute carnage
> Hatred for hatred, stray bullets and more.[47]

The group advocates more peace and understanding between men, but they side with the Palestinian people whom they consider to be the oppressed group as opposed to the Israeli conquerors. The song ends with a clarification by the group:

> If in your opinion we are taking sides, you have to understand
> We are not speaking as Muslims
> Only as human beings.[48]

Therefore, Sniper does not wish to be seen as a group whose members support the Palestinian because of their Muslim faith, but simply because they are – like any individuals – external observers of the conflict. We might nevertheless notice that the treatment of this current topic comes together with an assertion of their personal religious belongings; for the listener, an obvious link is made between their selecting and treating such a theme, and the religious beliefs of the members of the group.

We should note that although Sniper does mention the war between the USA and Iraq, the Israeli–Palestinian conflict is the only international conflict which forms the subject of an entire song. This indicates a particular interest in this conflict, but we cannot therefore conclude that there is a direct link with the religious beliefs of the members of the group.

Therefore, if some clues can show us that the international political and religious context can have an effect on the treatment of religion in French rap lyrics, nothing in the lyrics themselves can allow us to be completely certain of this point of view.

Does religion appear in the rap as a form of reaction against French society? Can the way French society deals with and treats the question of religion and of Islam be a reason for the increase in the religious speech in rap music?

Nothing in the texts analysed indicates that the religious line, partly Muslim, in French rap music cannot be explained as a reaction by the Muslim community, or any other religious community, to the attitude of the French State or French society to all religions.

However, the link which could be made between the development of the religious line in rap and the functioning of French society can be understood in another way.

We have observed that five of the productions analysed deal with religion. Yet, the rappers who take up the theme of religion are also the ones whose speech is anchored in the life of the French underprivileged areas. The six artists who according to their lyrics have religious beliefs also present themselves as 'the sad heirs of the strict truth'[49] (Booba) whose association with the poorer areas in France is either clearly stated: 'I come from the ghetto'[50] (113), 'I'm from the suburbs, you can sense that from afar'[51] (Kery James), or hinted at in their textual productions through the use of the pronoun 'we' whenever the rapper describes life on poor French estates.

On the contrary, the absence of a religious type of speech can be observed in the other artists' productions (Triptik, Svinkels, TTC, Oxmo Puccino, NTM and Assassin); they do not set their speech within the context of suburbs or underprivileged areas – except for the old school groups NTM and IAM – and they do not refer to the world of the deprived estates in a descriptive way. If any reference to this world is ever made, it is usually critical. Here the rapper Dabaaz, from the Triptik group, addresses a youth from the deprived estates:

> Since you've been smoking, you only like Colts; you swim
>   your own crawl
> Burn the car, take your buildings for the Pentagon
> You only feed stats, vandalising stadiums
>
> The more you do, the more you turn those fascists on.[52]

We can then observe a link between the religious and Muslim speech of the rapper and the suburban origins of the rappers. This link can be understood in different ways.

For rappers, and for the inhabitants of the French suburbs, choosing a religion can be considered a way of reversing a 'social stigma'. According to Erving Goffman (1977), religion enables one to reverse the social, political and economic domination this population endures. The individual then only has to explain himself to God, and no one else. In this way it is no longer the gaze of the other which is essential in the building of one's individual identity, but God's gaze. Religion allows a transcendence of social reality, but it also allows a reversal of the domination relationship: the individual is not dominated by man any more, but by God, who dominates the whole of humanity. This quest for the reversal of social stigma finds an effective medium in religion. This means that the quest for equality (all men will be submitted to divine will), or for the reversal of domination, goes through a spiritual belief and not through a quest for social equality by means of political and social struggles.

As sociologist Samir Amghar has expressed it:

> the march of the Arabs in 1983[53] and the struggle for integration led by older brothers were experienced by the second and third generation youths as a failure . . . The only utopia in the utopias market is Islam, not trade-unionism.[54]

The religious faith of some of the French rappers (essentially Muslim, as we have seen) has to be understood as a reaction against the acknowledgement of failure of integration and social struggles on behalf of which rap pioneers spoke out. The reactions expressed in rap productions reveal, then, the despair and the absence of desire to struggle, politically and socially, among the young people in deprived areas because

> in a way, the belonging to religious values is a symmetry of the detachment from the activist spirit. It is a sociological constant: whenever the constraints of social order are experienced as an inescapable fatality, the subject, who is conscious of being powerless to change the world, tends to turn away from the action and willingly turns to religion which, in its own way, legitimates the unjustifiable by painting in glowing colours the hope for a promising beyond. (Béthune 2004)

The allusion to religion has to be apprehended as the sign of the appearance of a form of renunciation on the part of the youths of the French ghetto of the possibilities to acquire – through social and political struggle – the rights they feel deprived of.[55] The speech of the rappers who adopt a religious line admittedly criticises the French political organisation (the French political class and some institutions such as the police) but it does not deal with politics as a vehicle of social struggle (Booba, Rohff, 113, Fonky Family, Kery James); or if it does, as in the case of Sniper, it is only to note with pessimism the failure of the previous social and political struggles.

For sociologist Samir Amghar, 'choosing Islam, which is a majority [religion] in the suburbs, and a strong and manly religion, has something of a protest in it which is identical to the rap music'; religious belief would then be a vehicle of social protest in itself, a way of constructing an identity, whether individual or collective, for French youths born of immigrant parents. It also constitutes a form of protest against the dominant social order. In addition, for this sociologist, the characteristics of the Muslim religion seem to be appropriate to the conditions of practice of the 'rap' activity. Religious belief can also be understood – paradoxically – as the new instrument of social struggle, an instrument to unite underprivileged French youths, represented by some of the rappers.

Religious belief would then allow the children born of immigrants to build up an individual and collective identity (an identity strengthened through meeting other youths, but also through family traditions) which would protest against the dominant French social (and religious) order. It would then be a medium of integration into the suburbs' social life, and at the same time it would enable the construction of an identity opposed to French society.

It is interesting to consider that, if religion today has become a factor of identification between the rap artist and his receiver, as well as a factor of social integration and identity construction for those same rappers and their listeners, it is because hip hop music and its values do not guarantee the function of integration that were attributed to it when French rap originally began.

The analysis of the rap texts shows that rappers who adopt a religious discourse do not deal with the hip hop theme at all, except for the group Fonky Family, who glorify hip hop as a form of 'street art'. In contrast, the non-religious productions of the other artists devote a part of their speech to hip hop in its entirety, and not only to rap.

Religion within rap music: a medium of social integration or separatism?

Our dissertation work enabled us to observe that artists anchored in the reality of the deprived French estates who adopt a religious type of speech have an audience predominantly from the working class, as opposed to the other rappers whose audience comprises more middle- and upper-class members. As regards productions, the boundary we can observe between those using religious speech and the others must be viewed in the perspective of the diversification of the productions of French rap, but also the diversification of the rap audience in France.

For the popular audience of French rap, the religious theme developed by some rappers belonging to the same social reality as they do may constitute a powerful factor of recognition and identification. This is not the case, however, for the middle- and upper-class audience of rap music, who find it more difficult to identify and to recognise themselves in the words of some rappers. This idea clearly appears in an article devoted to Kery James's album *Knowing and Living Together*, which was published on an Internet website specialising in rap music:

> the feeling of a recurring moralising quickly becomes painful.
> Indoctrination is not far away. Both CDs examined closely,
> there's only one feeling left: this *Knowing and living together*

could have been *Knowing and living together among Muslims*. How can we not have this thought when listening to some words of Kery: 'What is becoming of our community? How many lost their ways? Left it? The Devil took possession of them. A plague on them! But who is our declared enemy? Him who separated some from Islam (*Science, a light*)'.[56] We might confess that in this state of mind and this affirmed Manichaeism, it may be difficult to reach knowledge and teach us how to live together, all together.[57]

If, for some rappers and their audience, religious speech enables social integration, it can also be considered as a sign of the demarcation and division between, on the one hand, French rap productions, and, on the other hand, the French rap audience as a whole.

Conclusion

The growth of the French rap scene was accompanied by the emergence of new tendencies within the French scene. At the beginning of French rap music, the commitment to hip hop values, which we can consider a religious form distinguishing the sacred from the profane, was a powerful medium of social integration for the rappers and the hip hop adherents (artists and receivers). However, the recent evolution of French rap tends to show that neither involvement in a discipline of hip hop, nor belief in its values, nor the form of social and political struggle it implies, are today factors of recognition or identification among French rap producers, their productions, and their receivers.

The analysis of the treatment of religion in current French rap music is one of the keys to understanding the evolution of the French rap scene and its audience. If the religious topic is today close to the 'street rap', rap which re-transcribes the world of the French suburbs and in which a part of the audience recognises itself, it takes away another part of the audience from those same productions. The boundary between these two types of audience seems to constitute a difference of social background, of social class, more than a difference of religion. It is through the consideration of 'popular' productions of French rap music, intended for a 'popular' audience, that the analysis of religion within French rap becomes meaningful.

7

Why didn't the Churches Begin to Burn a Thousand Years Earlier?[1]

Gry Mørk

A religion's sacred buildings stand as symbols of that particular religion's authoritative system of values and, insofar as we are dealing with a state religion, those of society as well. These buildings are therefore sometimes targets for oppositional individuals and groupings in their protests against society and their expression of identity (Hetherington 1998: 72, 105ff.). To some people Christian churches, chapels and cathedrals stand as provocative, manifest and constant reminders of the Christian tradition's illegitimate entrenchment, centuries-long presence, and deep cultural and social influence. This is true in Norway and other countries around the world, and between 1992 and 1998 about 50 Christian sacred buildings were torched in Norway.

The burning of the Holmenkollen chapel, which was known as the royal family's preferred church, and the Methodist church in Sarpsborg, where a fireman lost his life, received massive media publicity. It was probably the 1992 arson attack on the Fantoft stave church that attracted the greatest attention from both the public and the media, however. The church was allegedly burnt down by a member of Norway's black metal scene, which at the time was both tiny and very extreme (Alver 1993: 2f; Mørk 82ff). The stave church had enormous social and religious, as well as economic and cultural value. It was one of Norway's oldest churches, exemplifying excellent local and artistic workmanship and building techniques, as well as a material expression of the transition from paganism to Christianity. The stave church was widely recognised as a national treasure. Not only did the Fantoft arson initiate a series of church burnings, but rumours spread that the man behind the act also had plans to blow up Nidarosdomen, the medieval cathedral in the city of Trondheim. It has never been established whether these rumours had any foundation.

The burning of churches is not limited to Norway, but has also taken place in neighbouring countries such as Sweden, Finland and Russia, as well as in other parts of the world, e.g. Britain, South America, Japan and Australia.

Even though there are bands within the black metal genre that have chosen a Christian profile, a varying degree of calculated antipathy towards Christianity existed – and still exists – as a premise, or framework for the creation and performance of this specific type of music and adherence to the scene connected to it (Mørk 2002, 2005).

The freeing of the individual

Christianity's position as state religion has meant that the boundaries between its religious, ideological and political functions are hazy and shifting. Although traditional values are constantly being challenged in Western societies, Christianity is still an influential part of these societies, and for this reason it affects the lives of the citizens of Western societies in various ways whether they like it or not. In Norway, and many other countries, Christian norms and values still pervade domains of society other than merely the religious one, e.g. the judicial and educational systems. Black metal is deeply concerned with individuation and differentiation, and therefore with the autonomy of the individual; hence it is on many levels an expression of the opposition between the individual and the system (Mørk 2005). Informant 'A', who was interviewed by Norwegian journalist Torstein Grude for a TV documentary on black metal,[2] thinks that a part of the point of burning churches was to 'get rid of that type of institution [the Christianity of the State church], and re-establish Norway as a Heathen country'. 'A' points out that he is against any form of organised religion, and that one of the main reasons for setting churches on fire was to make a stand against the institutionalisation of religion and the religious concentration of power that it led to. Informant 'C' speaks of his own motive for setting a church on fire in the following manner:

> [A]ll the time Norway has to be moral. The Christian morality in Norway always has to be followed, rules, laws, everything has to be religious, and the more you think of Norway being Christian, the more you hate it. The more you realise that Norway never should have been Christianised; it should have been dechristianised a long time ago. And that's really the point I made by burning [x] church, to stress that. It's really a very symbolic act. (Grude's material)

Vindkall, a member of the Swedish black metal band Domgård and a convicted church arsonist, has said that: 'Although most people don't care about religion today, they are still not free of a thousand-year moral indoctrination and degeneration' (quoted in Losten 2001: 124). He continues: 'I have a totally different moral philosophy than that which is forced upon you at school – society's initial process of indoctrination' (ibid.). At the same time he dismisses the idea that his family and upbringing have anything to do with his hostility towards Christianity and contemporary society (Losten 2001: 120). Instead he explains his contempt of the Judaeo-Christian tradition and humanism by claiming to have had a strong fascination for the evil and the eerie, which he preferred to the good and the safe ever since childhood, in addition to emphasising the fact that he grew up in 'a Christian society with sick laws that have attempted to deprave my Self and my creativity' (ibid.). Vikernes, with his band Burzum, also criticises Christianity's universal pretension and idea of its own infallibility. In general a member of the black metal scene may be seen as an example of the late-modern human being who wants to perceive, think and live on their own terms, and who trusts their own experiences instead of institutionally based, lifeless dogmas. There is an urge towards strong, dangerous and extreme living – through burning churches, for instance, or through the cutting and burning of one's own flesh, playing effervescent and brutal music, worshipping the macabre. In other words, a vital impetus behind church burnings has been a revolt against Christianity's hegemonic interpretations of life, the expression of a wish to make visible and loosen or burst what the arsonists consider to be this religion's strong grip on the free, creative individual: the 'original' or 'authentic' human being, culture and society. Gaahl, the main member of the Norwegian black metal band Trelldom and singer in the notorious band Gorgoroth, claims that black metal essentially has to do with an uncompromising will never to submit to anything.

Remembering and reawakening heathen forces

'[T]he (hi)stories of the forgotten [are] now about to be remembered', the social anthropologist Thomas Hylland Eriksen writes (1996: 65).[3] In other words, the official, i.e. 'conqueror's', portrayals of history are being challenged to an increasing degree by alternative versions of history. The church arsons can be viewed as a result of this tendency. Within the black metal scene a multitude of alternative versions of history – which question and criticise the way the Christianising of the Germanic areas is presented as liberation from 'the darkness' of heathenism – are being consumed, reproduced and transformed. From the early years of (Norwegian) black metal's development in 1991/92, some Norwegian bands began to incorporate elements from the Norse tradition as part of the genre's prominent orientation towards the past and that which is ancient, and as an addition or alternative to concepts, symbols and ideas of a more satanic type. There is a prevailing view within the black metal scene that the Nordic countries, and for that matter Northern Europe or the whole of the Germanic cultural area, should never have been Christianised. The pagan, non-Christian past is perceived as a time of greatness in various different ways, while the Christianisation of 'the North' is thought to have inaugurated an era or process of degeneration which has continued until the present day (Mørk 2002). The former black metal musician Varg Vikernes, one of the founders of the black metal scene, is serving the longest prison sentence possible under Norwegian law, convicted of and sentenced for first-degree murder, church arsons and vandalising graveyards, among other things. He likes to see the 6 June 1992 burning of Fantoft stave church in the light of what historically is set as the starting point of the Viking age: the attack on Lindisfarne monastery:

> If one looks at history, then you see that the Viking age
> begins with Vikings attacking the monastery on Lindisfarne,

that is The Holy Island outside England, and burning the monastery and killing the monks, and that was the 6th of June. According to other sources it was the 8th of June . . . [One] thinks they were Vikings from Hordaland in Norway. Then Fantoft stave church burned the 6th of June, the same date in Hordaland as [Lindisfarne]. (Grude's material)

Another, unknown Norwegian black metal informant has said: 'Some may think it a wrong way to damage Christianity, but at that time it wasn't a wrong way. Perhaps the beginning' (Grude's material). The 'attack' on Fantoft was in other words perhaps meant to start a new 'Viking age', a new heathen era. I might also add that black metal lyrics often depict apocalyptic visions of some sort or other, where of course the lyrical subjects represent the 'dark' side or mighty, aggressive 'Heathen' forces (Mørk 2002). Good examples of this are the following lyric excerpts taken from work by the bands Darkthrone and Immortal:

Horned Master of Endless Time / Summon thy Unholy Disciples [. . .] / Gather on the highest Mountain / United by Hatred / The final Superjoint Ritual [. . .] / The Pagan Winter / Kept for the Obscure [. . .] / For this Eternal Winter / A New God Ruled the Sky [. . .]

(excerpt from 'The Pagan Winter' from Darkthrone's album *A Blaze In The Northern Sky*, 1992)

North black hordes storms through invincible cyclones of frostwinds / I lift my hands and join the ceremonial circle of one wind / Eyes of stone now sleeps into eternal night / This winter is forever / A wind of red I rode / A wind of evil cold [. . .] / A perfect vision of the rising Northland

(excerpt from 'A Perfect Vision Of The Rising Northland' from Immortal's album *Diabolical Fullmoon Mysticism*, 1992)

Black metal's use of the Norse tradition reveals a national romantic attitude. The cultural historian Arne Engelstad (2001: 12) describes national romanticism as a part of the Romantic movement of the nineteenth century, 'which in many ways combines . . . both the left-wing romanticism oriented towards the future with its demand for national independence and right-wing romanticism oriented towards the past with its concern with the history and ancient culture of the people'. Norse black metal and the parts of the scene that relate to the Norse tradition have traits in common with both right- and left-wing romanticism, and may therefore be branded national romantic. Black metal attends to the retrospective character of right-wing romanticism with its orientation towards wild and untouched nature, together with the longing for a time of origin when man lived authentically. At the same time, it embodies the progressivism, the revolutionary motif of liberation, of left-wing romanticism.

The church arsons are nevertheless in general, at least in retrospect, deemed as symbolic acts. 'A' sees it as unlikely that anyone seriously believed that it would be possible to restore heathenism (Grude's material). When speaking of the church arsons Vikernes admits it is not very realistic that a crowd of youths could possibly 'clear the heathen soil of Europe of church buildings. That would have been a full-time occupation of many years, because there are so many. They have spread those buildings in every little corner of the whole of Europe' (Grude's material).

The pagan ancestor's avengers

In the Norse black metal community the Viking era is represented as Scandinavia's Golden Age – especially when it comes to the more belligerent, masculine, heroic and 'dark' aspects of it – and the Norse way of life is seen as natural and right for people from the northern part of Europe. Honour, strength, pride and courage were core values within the black metal scene – drive, hard-heartedness and youthful, uncompromising idealism were signs that one was brave, manly and worthy of respect. In line with this and the worship of – or at least the acceptance of – strife, aggression, violence, chaos and war, to a certain degree inspired by the Norse male and warrior ideal and the code of honour and revenge of the Vikings, an adamant eye-for-an-eye and tooth-for-a-tooth ethics was applied. In the knowledge that Christianity was forced upon the Viking ancestors, often brutally and against their will, one of the propelling forces behind church arsons has been a sense of revenge: 'The way I see it, there is of course a kind of motive of revenge present, where the church gets to taste its own medicine. The church has forced itself forward in such a despicable, cowardly and brutal way in Norway that it is unbelievable', says Vikernes (Grude's material). Members of the Swedish black metal scene who have been imprisoned for church arsons also claim revenge as a motive (Losten 2001: 115). Apologies or expressions of regret and bad conscience on the part of church arsonists, and condemnations of such acts by members of the scene in general, are hard to find, although it must be said that opinions differ about the burning of Fantoft stave church, which to a certain extent contained pagan cultural elements. In addition to this, some members of the scene have for different reasons distanced themselves from or criticised the church arsons, but not out of sympathy with the Christians or because of any moral scruples about them. One of the reasons given is that they distract people from the heart of the scene, the music, which is the most important thing. Another reason is that the risk one runs in burning a church is not worthwhile. It is seen as quite stupid to risk being put in prison and run into bottomless debt in order to make a personal statement against a world view and religious institution that it is impossible to get rid of anyway, as shown by the rebuilding of the churches. However, some very recent examples of the open-minded attitude towards church arsons are statements made by Jørn Inge Tunsberg from the band Hades Almighty, who has served a prison sentence for having participated in the burning of Åsane church in Bergen, and Gaahl, both in the 2005 documentary 'Metal – A Headbanger's Journey' by Sam Dunn and Scot McFadyen. Gaahl supports church burning 100 per cent and claims that it will be done more frequently in the future, and Tunsberg says that he has always stood for and will always stand for this act. Vikernes interprets the condemnation of the burning of Christianity's sacred buildings as just another instance of the double standard of Christians, their attempts at manipulation and lust for power:

> they say that it was a thousand years ago, and that times have changed – that's just another way of saying 'It's permitted to kill when we do the killing, but when we have killed the ones that we want to kill, it's not allowed to kill anymore'. (Grude's material)

In any event, the contempt for the Judaeo-Christian tradition must have reached explosive levels given the extreme emphasis on being 'true' which prevailed within the Norwegian black metal scene for a period of time: music, everyday life and 'teachings' should be one. Action should follow artistic expression and the attitudes it embodied. One was supposed to *be* black metal. One was supposed to be *true* (Bossius 2003; Mørk 2002, 2005).

In black metal the old or ancient is cherished at the expense of the new and modern. This has not, however, prevented the burning of old Christian churches, because 'the old' or 'ancient' is primarily related to the heathen age or heathen culture, meaning the 'pre-Christian' or 'non-Christian'. Besides, combating Christianity in all its manifestations has had a higher priority than preserving something just because of its extreme age. The Swede Vindkall, and his companion Illbrand, probably knew prior to the deed that the church they set on fire was very old. 'Since I am hostile towards Christianity and the church, it seems obvious that I am indifferent to the age of my enemy's temples', Vindkall says, and continues: 'Bäckaby church would most probably have been done away with regardless of our knowledge of its age' (Losten 2001: 119). 'A' emphasises that even though some of the churches can be seen as beautiful buildings, national treasures and historical monuments, this is a one-sided, warped perspective that too easily makes us forget that Christianity was introduced in Norway in a manner which would not be tolerated anywhere in the world today. 'A' also underlines that the things that existed in Norway before Christianity arrived and was established, also ought to be regarded as national treasures (Grude's material).

According to several members of the black metal scene the local – pre-Christian or non-Christian – religion and culture were desecrated, suppressed, and immorally and illegally driven away. The introduction of Christianity at the expense of pagan beliefs and customs is viewed as sacrilege, the erection of churches as desecration of native soil. Or as Vindkall puts it: 'Christian churches and other buildings of non-Nordic cultures disgrace our land, our heritage' (Losten 2001: 124).[4] A rage smoulders within parts of the scene over the fact that the sacred places of the pagan ancestors were ruined and obliterated by the Christians, and that churches were often built on top of or near these sacred places as a strategy in the Christianisation process. One of the explanations given by Vikernes for the burning of Fantoft stave church was that it was built 'in the middle of an old, heathen sacred place, where there was a natural circle and a *horg*. A *horg* is a heathen temple, a mound of stone, where sacrifices were made. And on top of this a church was placed' (Grude's material). The idea seems to be that with their churches the Christians occupied – and continue to occupy – places of power throughout the Norwegian landscape. These are called 'places of power' because the circle is a well-known ancient occult symbol and because these specific places are believed to have served as ritual spaces in the pre-Christian age. Vikernes continues:

> Christianity is the most arrogant, most loathsome creature that has ever come to this land. Not only have they eradicated our culture, they have even built their churches on top of the ruins of our old temples, and then they come and tell us that we cannot tear them down because they are protected heritage sites! By so doing they have closed off, they have denied us any possibility of getting in touch with our culture, because they have protected that which stands on top. (Ibid.)

In any case, the linking of the Vikings' attack on Lindisfarne monastery and modern Norwegians' attack on the stave church at Fantoft – or the linking of Norse Heathenism to the burning of churches in general – may have reinforced the motivation for such acts and is likely to have added a certain historic air or sense of grandeur and a 'religious' aura to the deed.

The creative power of fire

The aggression, the violence, directed towards Christianity, here concretised through church burning, is a form of counter-violence; a creative, vengeful violence in that it can be seen as a reaction to the illegitimate, violent display of power the Christians have used throughout history in order to assert control over people of other beliefs and practices. As Gorgoroth writes on the sleeve of the album *Destroyer* (1998):

> The sight of burning churches, it fills our hearts with joy. The fanfares, they are resounding – the earth is booming from

the sound. We are marching through the streets in step. The Plague is cast back by force.

The Norwegian philosopher Knut Kolnar refers to the philosopher Frantz Fanon's reflections on violence as a primary strategy for people seeking liberation from oppressive forces. The cleansing and renewing potential of violence gives it a crucial function in the eradication of the marks that the oppressors have impressed on people's bodies and minds, so that the rebuilding of the pride, dignity and independence of the self can take place (Kolnar 2003: 80). The burning of buildings sacred to Christians must have been connected with extraordinary states of mind and sensational experiences before, during, and/or after the act. Descriptions of this type of act relate it for instance to a need to express and discharge anger and hatred (Grude's material; Losten 2001: 115). Vindkall states that he still remembers 'the nights of the fires with pride and grand arrogance', and he, who was 19 or 20 years old when the church was set on fire in 2000, adds: 'I think you understand that this is not some kind of random juvenile prank, for that I am five years too old' (Losten 2001: 115; 119).

Flames and fire have throughout history been symbols of suffering and destruction, but also of purification and power. A church collapsing under the power of flames may have worked as a powerful metaphor of Christianity's breakdown in society. Burning down a church may also be a 'sensuously' symbolic way of eradicating any traces of Christianity that might be left within oneself, as well as indicating a final break with the dominant cultural and social environment. But fire's regenerative and 'creative' aspects reveal themselves in the case of forest fires, where some time after a devastating fire the forest floor starts to sprout again. For Vikernes too, destruction and creation/construction are two sides of the same coin, or put a bit differently, the symbol of flames and fire is complex and flexible, its meaning dependent on the context in which it is being used. One of Vikernes's goals with his one-man band Burzum has been enlightenment (Mørk 2002). He wanted

> to awaken in people's soul something that has lain fallow for nearly a thousand years. I wish to throw dry twigs and new wood on the embers smouldering beneath the ashes of the soul of the people, so that Odin's fire can begin to burn again.

So that the Norse flames can lick towards the sky again.
(Vikernes, letter dated 29 February 2000)

This statement, which metaphorically reveals something about the motivation behind the musical creativity, not only indirectly reveals his opinion of Christianity as having burnt down the soul of the people, but also alludes to the church arsons from which flames literally licked up towards the sky and attracted the attention of people all over the world. An almost identical metaphor has been used by Vikernes in his accounts of the motivations behind church arsons, the Fantoft fire in particular. Vikernes explains that the point was to awaken or 'ignite' Odin and the vestiges of the pagan cast of mind in people's souls:

> The first church burned on the 6th of June [1992], with the intention probably to light a flame, to put dried grass and branches on that, to light it up on the coal and the fire to make it big. It's a psychological picture – an almost dead fire, a symbol of our heathen consciousness. The point was to throw dry wood and branches on that, to light it up and reach toward the sky again, as a growing force. That was the point, and it worked. (Vikernes in Moynihan and Søderlind 1998: 89)

Acts of violence may, from the standpoint of their perpetrator(s), have an overturning potential and goal, at the same time as having a 'cleansing', regenerating, structuring power or effect. In other words, they may carry both a 'dimension of revolution and hope' (Kolnar 2003: 231).

Incorporation of Norse Heathen identity

Norse Heathen beliefs and practices are conceived of as the appropriate and natural – the authentic – way of life for people of Scandinavian or Northern European origin, as they were a product of the symbiotic relationship between the natural environment and the inhabitants of the land. The Christianisation of the Northern countries is viewed – and to a certain degree *felt* or *experienced* – as a brutal and systematic encroachment on its native inhabitants and even on the own individual Self. This is due partly to the fact that the identification with the Norse ancestors and cultural tradition in (Norse) black metal is expressed and made vivid through what I have called 'live-the-part' identification (Mørk 2002). Within the black metal scene the Vikings may be spoken of as if one is a Viking oneself, participates in their ventures or is an incarnation of some kind of Viking spirit. The following statement by Vikernes exemplifies this proximate, vivid form of identification:

> [W]e did not at all have Christianity here any earlier; on the contrary we embarked on Viking expeditions much earlier than assumed . . . My conclusion is that yes, we were and still are hostile towards strangers. Or perhaps the Romans' fear of *Furor Teutonicus* (Germanic fury) and the Europeans' fear of the wrath of the Normans is based on our courtesy towards them? (Vikernes, letter dated 29 February 2000)

Use of concepts and metaphors related to kinship (i.e. 'ancestors', 'forefathers', 'son of Odin') and botany (i.e. 'roots'), as well as possessive pronouns such as 'our' or 'ours' when referring to the heathen ancestors and the Norse cultural heritage, is also quite common. All in all, this connects the Norse ancestors and tradition to private memories, to intimate and important experiences from one's own life, which makes it emotionally weighty, and contributes to the development of a heathen self-perception and sense of belonging together by activating a feeling of commitment and loyalty (Eriksen 1996: 50, 54f).

It is, however, a fact that the church arsonists are a minority within the black metal scene and that some, although few, take a stand against such acts. But in the case of those who sympathise with church burning and those who have set churches on fire or will do so in the future, this phenomenon and its intra-scenic interpretation will play a part in the formation of their self-perception. We 'are' the stories we tell about ourselves. Not only are the church arsons understood as actions rooted in an attachment to Norse Heathendom, but it is likely that their ability to induce strong physical reactions furthers the formation, incorporation and corroboration of a Norse identity. It is important to note, however, that the church arsons are only part of a wider landscape of revitalisation in the context of black metal. The aesthetic dimension dealing with image and musical activity have a far greater significance than church arsons. The music is the core that everything else revolves around. Fusing old, pre- or non-Christian elements of tradition with such an expressive and impressive form of music as black metal – a form that is even perceived by some as a channelling or reawakening of heathen forces or a Norse fury – may be seen to make the Norse cultural heritage even more powerful in relation to the identity processing. Altogether the connection that is established between the music, the image, the church arsons and the Norse tradition enhances the Norse identification and contributes to the creation of existential meaning. The Norse era becomes more real, more present, and more than just a distant, meaningful past for which one keeps longing. People who identify with the culture and people of the Norse era and forge this into their own life story, even acting on the basis of such a relationship, see themselves as becoming some kind of Viking, or even a figure from Norse mythology such as an *ås* or *åsynje* (god or goddess), *jotun* (giant), depending on how strong the identification is. Gaahl, for instance, perceives himself as a son of Odin, and I personally know a woman connected with the scene who thinks of herself as a daughter of Odin. It is very unlikely that these two are the only ones within the black metal scene who relate to the Norse tradition in this manner.

Restoration and framing of authentic manhood

The black metal community is a male community. It was developed by older boys and young men for themselves as well as for like-minded people of the same sex, in a phase of life when shaking themselves free of parents and other authorities, and finding their own identity and place in society are of the utmost importance (see also Bossius 2003).[5] Members of the early black metal scene were also almost desperate to distance themselves from 'the kids' in the underground and more mainstream metal scene. This underlines the point that this is a movement about older boys and young men emerging from childhood into the adult world with its many laws, commitments and responsibilities, as well as liberties and rights, in a global society where manliness has become something unclear, fragmented and shifting (Mørk 2005). This understanding of the black metal scene as an expressive 'cult' of masculinity is strengthened by its conveyance of sexist attitudes, such as a patronising view of women, a traditional view on gender roles, and a rejection of 'feminine' values. All this is combined with the near-impossibility for girls to be accepted as equal members of a scene overflowing with traditionally masculine identity markers. Homosexuality is very often frowned upon, and the scene is furthermore (to a greater or lesser degree) hierarchically structured. It is fascinated by violence and a variety of grotesque phenomena, and the various symbols to which the self-image is tied are often very masculine in nature (Mørk 2002, 2005). A gendered perspective may thus be fruitful in analysing this subculture since the construction, shaping and corroboration of masculine identity – conceived of as authentic and natural manliness – is one of its most distinctive features.

Pain and violence have been central ingredients in manhood rites in various cultures throughout history, and war and violence are historically speaking linked to men and often considered to be part of the cultivation of masculinity (Kolnar 2003: 202). In the song 'War' on Burzum's album *Burzum*, music-making is fundamentally related to such issues:

> This is War / I lie Wounded on Wintery Ground / With Hundred of Corpses around / Many Wounded Crawl Helplessly around / On the Blood Red Snowy Ground / War / Cries of the (ha, ha) suffering sound / Cries for help to all their dear Moms / War / Many hours of music / Many drops of blood / Many shiverings and now I am dead / And still we must never give up / War.

This unvarnished depiction of a wintry battlefield reveals a lack of compassion for its suffering and helpless victims. Although he is in the same boat as the others on the battlefield, the lyrical subject seems insensitive or indifferent even to his own misery, and also refuses to succumb to his own suffering. The parallel that is being drawn between the battlefield scenario and playing music also reveals the existential scope of this dark form of art. Black metal is said by several musicians to be at the very core of their being, inseparably tied to their lives and who they are (Mørk 2005). The black metal scene's critique of Judaeo-Christian dualism (or any other fundamentally dualistic religion, ideology and philosophy) reflects alternative experiences and judgements of 'darkness', of what its absence as well as presence mean for the development and quality of life of men, of people and sometimes even the human race. This is clearly presented in the lyrics of 'Snu mikrokosmos tegn' (i.e. 'Turn the sign of micro cosmos') on the 1992 Burzum album *Det som engang var* ('What once was'). This song also exemplifies another typical pattern within black metal: the visual and lyrical representation of 'darkness' and nature (or 'dark' nature) as providing power and energy:

> No silence out here – / a dream / Here where the moon reigns – / a dream / I hate this wood / where no danger threatens / No wolf / no bear / no troll / is breathing / No evil spirits / nothing / is breathing / Just the night and I – / just the night and I / One night I will go to Hell.

In this song, which clearly displays the influence of the fantasy genre on the world of Burzum, the longing for 'Hell' is brought to life or accentuated within the framework of safe and empty nocturnal scenery. 'Hell' represents a vibrant and dynamic existence, seething from the interplay between contrasting forces, where vigilance, pulse and immediate self- and life-presence is made possible by its unpredictable, challenging and hazardous nature. This is not the only song by Burzum that deals with a subject of this kind (see for example 'What once were' [1992] on the album carrying the truly expressive title *If the light catches us*); nor is Burzum the only band that deals with this kind of subject matter. A fulfilling existence depends on the inclusion of 'darkness' in the life-world of humans, which the Burzum song 'Decrepitude' on *Filosofem* (1992) depicts with the utmost clarity:

> When night falls / she cloaks the world / in impenetrable darkness / A chill rises / from the soil / and contaminates the air / suddenly . . . / life has new meaning.

The darkness and shuddering chill of the night revitalises life. It is quite possible to interpret the scenario in 'Snu mikrokosmos tegn' as a young man's vision of what it takes to fully realise his masculine potential, while still having to live in a world where this – the release of violent and virile energy – is absent, illegitimate. The worship of 'darkness', its multifaceted stress on aggression (i.e. the obsession with weapons) and critical existential experiences that more generally are imparted by the black metal scene can thus fruitfully be viewed as a response to serious challenges that confront contemporary, Western males in regard to the formation of masculine identity and existential meaning. In a black metal context Christianity and its dualism are viewed as the main cause of man having been disrupted and alienated from his natural state of being and natural wholesomeness.

Christianity as a destroyer of manhood

Many black metal bands have been influenced by Burzum's judgement of the Judaeo-Christian tradition as a spiritual plague, i.e. as a warped and mentally deranged view of life. In Darkthrone's song 'En vind av sorg' ('A wind of sorrow') on the album *Panzerfaust* (1994) 'Christian man's blood' is similarly described as 'leeches on our hearts'. According to the black metal scene, Christianity, because of its dualism, has gone a long way towards banishing and demonising dark, shady and 'evil' drives, forces and powers within the universe and man, and towards stigmatising violence as a means of expression. This is seen to make redundant the male subject's specifically masculine resources; to choke his natural drive towards masculine fullness and dignity. In other words, Christianity is seen as offering an effeminising view and way of life. The destructive effect that Christian dualism is thought to have on male individuals is harshly suggested in the piece 'Musstad' on Burzum's album *Filosofem*:

> With the spiritual plague [the light] from the south came also that which killed courage and honour . . . Men that could have won glory and honour by dying a worthy death on the battlefield were forced to die of old age. The forces of darkness were to be weeded out, war was a sin and no man was ever to kill another. Peace prevailed, but no true peace, because the peace depleted people's powers more than any war might have depleted them, for eternal peace is no peace, it is the differences that create energy. The light did not warm them, but burnt them, the light did not let them see, it bedazzled them, the light sucked out all their energy, and they died in bed after a long, honourless life. The light brought them peace, God's peace, true Hell. (My translation)

Manliness is here linked to the Norse tradition and its gender ideals. The male Viking represents paradigmatic and traditional masculinity; he is an image of what it really means to be a man and of the type of cultural values that are necessary if men are to fully realise their potential (Sægrov 1996). In general the Norse references and symbols used in black metal are characteristically masculine. Mjølner – i.e. the hammer of the god Tor (Thor) – and the warrior god Odin are very common symbols, not to mention the use of the iron cross, and the fascination with the *berserkr* and the *einherjr*,[6] both warrior elites. A fairly direct portrayal of Jesus (a male(!) figure and symbol of Christianity) as a dark, cold and life-extinguishing figure or force, irreconcilable with vitality and natural life, is found in the lyrics of the song 'Jesu død' (i.e. 'Jesus' death') on Burzum's album *Filosofem* (1993):

> A figure was lying on the ground / so evil that the flowers about withered / a gloomy soul was lying on the ground / so cold that all the water turned to ice / Then a shadow dropped over the wood // when the soul of the figure faded away / because the soul of the figure was a shadow / a shadow of the force of evil.

As stigmatisation, tabooing and discrediting of man's – or rather, the male subject's – 'dark' sides is regarded as having made him into a divided being, a stranger to himself, the black metal worship of 'darkness' is intended to make man whole again, restore man's kinship with nature; in other words, to return him to his natural state of being. The realisation of true masculinity through exploring 'the forces of darkness', warfare and killing, is not related to the Norse cultural tradition and the heathen ancestors alone, but, as already suggested, is also seen as a natural process. The cultural historian Nina Witoszec (1998: 17) has claimed that Norway's natural heritage has served for centuries as a very strong symbol of identity for Norwegians, sometimes to the degree that the images of nature and 'Norwegian-ness' appear as nearly one and the same thing. According to Witoszec (1998: 11ff) this indicates an absorption of the strong and vivid Germanic-heathen 'identity fable' that Tacitus created through his romanticised depiction of the Germanic folk as a superior people of nature, whose brutality and belligerence stood in sharp contrast to the decadent and blasé elite of his time. She claims that Tacitus' writings generated perceptions of identity and nature as 'hierarchic, emotional and violent', which 'set Nature up against Reason' and has encouraged 'the swaggering personality who does not know his own limitations' (Witoszec 1998: 11ff). Within the black metal scene the perception of self is fundamentally and especially tied to the Norwegian climate and landscapes, and its majestic, harsh and wilful character is taken as a model of authentic being. Besides the extensive use of pure landscape pictures, it is also very common to do photo shoots in natural environments, thereby depicting the individual band member or the band as a whole as inserted or immersed in, or even as extensions of nature. There are many grim, gloomy and theatrical pictures of often wild and proud-looking band members posing in their black metal outfits – frequently carrying weapons of some old-fashioned and primitive kind such as swords, daggers, maces, axes and scythes[7] – preferably in the woods at night, sometimes in the winter. In song lyrics the lyrical subjects are occasionally depicted as incarnations of natural forces, often hunting or battling Christians. Darkthrone closely portrays the subjects in the song 'A Blaze in the Northern Sky' as a Northern storm's pride, 'a triumphant sight on a Northern Sky'. Another black metal band that has been greatly influenced by the mighty and inhospitable aspects of Norwegian scenery is Immortal, as shown in album titles such as *At the Heart of Winter* (1999) and *Sons of Northern Darkness* (2002).

It could be said that apart from lyrical and visual elements, this inspiration is reflected in the genre's distinctly clear and cold, fast, fresh and fierce music style. Sleeve and band photos as well as lyrical content, among other things, reveal the prevailing view within the black metal scene of what it means for humans – especially men – to be in a 'natural state'. Emotions and traits such as hatred, contempt, selfishness, arrogance, and vengefulness are to be cultivated. During a police interrogation an infamous member of the black metal scene explained that the waging of war is natural and great, that feelings of hatred, jealousy and wickedness are natural, innate, and ought to be released through aggression.[8]

Burning churches presumably leads to an experience of immediate and powerful masculine fulfilment and energy; and hence a formation and reinforcement of masculine identity. In addition to being gateways to extraordinary, transcendent bodily experiences and presence, such acts activate the ideal, traditional and essentialistic conceptions of manhood within the scene, as such conceptions are expressed and activated through demands for boldness or an ability to take action, self-confidence and wilfulness, as well as requiring courage and strength, a capacity for violence and endurance of pain – ideals and practices demanding mental and physical strength (Mørk 2005). The burning of churches realises and hence brings about the internalisation of the idea that the capacity to act evinces strong and authentic masculinity. The phrasing 'weak/cowardly men talk/threaten, strong/ real men act', the idealisation of action and standing by one's word, as well as the judgement of regret as an indication of weakness were, at least for a period of time, for quite a few members of the scene, very influential. This serves to show not only the limited value attributed to words, reason and dialogue within the scene, but also that these values had to do with establishing and expressing masculine identity. The stress that was placed on these values also signals that the masculine identity processing must have been of a quite urgent character.

The insufficiency of reason

Within black metal the body is in general given precedence as a field of expression, experience and knowledge. This is communicated through the centrality of the musical, visual and 'behavioural' aesthetic (or rather, anti-aesthetic), the emphasis on the individual's creative and counter-cultural ability to take action (his 'performing' abilities), through its holistic outlook, focus on aggression and passionate commitment as well as mystic/occult spirituality and practice (Mørk 2002, 2005). The complexity of the significance of the body in the context of black metal imparts a multi-layered cultural criticism of traditions that are seen as leading to the disintegration and alienation of man, and to a shallowness and demystification of existence. It can, for example, be seen as a strategy against or liberation from the Christian tradition's claim that the 'world of the flesh' is sinful, as well as its endeavour to indoctrinate people with its version of the truth. It may also convey a critical view on the somewhat one-sided appraisal of the mind, reason, intellect and empirical science within modernity. When bodily responses that exist separately from, prior to or beyond the limits set by reason are placed above words, dialogue, and cool, calm and collected rationality, they also function as primary and indispensable emancipatory strategies, especially for males. Kolnar (2003) is interested in how consumption has become something that people *are*, especially in regard to those who were born into and/or have grown up in postmodern consumer society, how aggression and extreme violence may be understood in relation to the consumerism of the contemporary, Western world. Consumption and consumerism are entangled in our whole mode of being – in our entire way or desiring, feeling, thinking, acting and choosing. And it is precisely for this reason, and because of the forceful and violent way it has been and is constantly being impressed into people's bodies and minds, that it has to be stopped and drained by way of 'wordless', e.g. aggressive, strategies: 'The words, the dialogue, the negotiations are only 'skin-deep', they are unable to transform the deep structures of identity [and patterns of world-cognition] that consumer society has imprinted' (Kolnar 2003: 201). Consumer culture has been, and in some senses still is, one of the greatest enemies of the black metal scene. However, it is not only consumerism that leads to 'wordless' strategies of this kind, but almost any structure, relation, religion, or ideology that is experienced as oppressive – such as Christianity – has the potential to do so. The church arsons exemplify this, and so does the significance of the body when it comes to change, articulation and consolidation of the self, as well as to the creation of existential meaning. The bodily domain possesses such a distinct and primary function with regard to the purification and restructuring of the self and its perception of the world because our body is what is most intimate to us, because we 'are' our body in the sense that we depend on it for our existence. We exist in the world through our body and also perceive the world through it. Kolnar maintains that 'it is via the transforming properties of violence that a homeless masculinity can establish a bodily and mental point of departure that enables a totally different and far more autonomous view of the cultural field and one's place in it' (Kolnar 2003: 203).

Summary

The multifaceted and uncompromising aggression that the black metal scene levels against Christianity can be seen as creative in the sense that it, as it is a response to what is conceived as this tradition's oppressive, hypocritical and alienating character, it has cleansing, liberating and reconstructive functions. The different ways in which the church arsons are linked to this severe antagonism towards the Judaeo-Christian tradition, but also to the identification with Norse Heathenism and the Viking ancestors, show that they have to do with identity processing; especially the formation, expression and corroboration of masculine identity conceived as authentic and natural. Christianity is in different ways and for different reasons regarded as blocking the process of individuation, not least masculine individuation.

The bodily domain is of the utmost importance within black metal, because the body is the primary source or arena of experience and expression for those seeking liberation from oppressive forces and the recreation of a new and independent view of self and the world.

8

21st-Century Trance Cult

Electronic dance music culture and its role in
replacing the traditional roles of religion
in Western European popular youth culture

Rupert Till

Introduction

This chapter explores the relationships between Electronic Dance
Music Culture (EDMC) and trance, religion, meaning and spirituality.
The term 'EDMC' is used because it describes a coherent group of
activities and cultural practices, including those in some nightclubs, at
free parties and festivals, and focuses on music genres such as trance,
techno, house and drum and bass, while excluding mainstream chart
music, rap and hip hop, which have different cultures. My work is
focused principally on England, although it resonates with and
relates to EDMC worldwide. As well as literature review, research
for this project has included 15 years spent between 1990 and 2005
participating in EDMC as a clubber, musician, DJ and event promoter.
Beginning with a perspective that was emic, my perspective developed
into participant observation, influenced by Chernoff's methodology.[1]
Research has included discussions with clubbers and event organisers,
and included attendance at numerous EDMC events and venues.
Many of these events were in the north of England, including those
in Sheffield (Headcharge, Planet Zogg, Destination Venus, Sundaze,
the Arches), York (Sweatbox, He La Hu), Leeds (The Warehouse,

The Gallery), as well as in Cambridge (Clueless), London, Manchester and at various music festivals and free parties. The cult of EDMC is a close-knit community, which is difficult to understand or penetrate unless one is within it, and I am indebted to those I met at these events for the information presented here.

It is within the trance music sub-genre of EDMC that overt religious references are most common, and so the trance music scene within EDMC is the focus here, although elements of religion and spirituality to some extent pervade EDMC in general. Many publications have investigated the relationships between religion, spirituality, meaning and EDMC. Clubbing has been shown to be meaningful for participants and to perform religious functions (Lynch 2005: 177), and clubbers are parts of neo-tribes, making fearless leaps into uncertainty (St John 2004: 19–45). EDMC is related to religious fete, or celebration (Gauthier 2004: 65–84), and can be regarded as implicit religion (Gauthier 2005). It exhibits many features of new religious movements, demonstrates socio-cultural revitalisation, and is highly meaningful and transformative (Olaveson 2004: 86). It is a 'secondary institution' (Lynch and Badger 2006), 'cultural religion' (Sylvan 2005), 'home' (Rietveld 1998), or 'temporary autonomous zone' (Bey 1985). It is clear that for those involved in EDMC it fulfils many of the functions traditionally served by religions, and that it bears many of the hallmarks and typical features of religion and spirituality.

Implicit and explicit religion in EDMC

During visits to EDMC events, I found many references to religious or spiritual elements. For example *The Celestine Prophecy* by James Redfield (1993) was a popular text amongst clubbers, and one that came up again and again in conversation. The book was a worldwide bestseller in the 1990s, and discusses spiritual insights and synchronicity. Through this book coincidental events were reified, imbuing clubbing with meaning and mystery. Some practised Reiki, healing, massage or reflexology in club 'chill out' rooms, often surrounded with spiritual imagery and paraphernalia referencing Buddhist, Taoist, Hindu or vaguely 'Eastern' spirituality, mixed up in a new age melting pot.

Clubs' 'chill out' rooms were places where clubbers could sit and talk, rest from dancing, or escape from the intensity of the main dance floor. For example, a monthly chill out club called Sundaze, based in Sheffield, was set up as a deliberate attempt to create a secular equivalent of a meditation or church event on Sunday nights, as a centre of culture and community for clubbers away from the frenzy of mainstream clubbing. Inspired by Frigid, a similar event in Sydney, Australia, Sundaze featured down-tempo music, video projections, art events, sofas and candles and targeted customers recovering from a weekend's clubbing before returning to work on Monday. The group developed links with a number of similar UK events and organisations, such as the Mellout, IDSpiral, Liquid Connective, Small World Stage and the annual Big Chill festival. These events had some artefacts reminiscent of religious organisations, and other similarities to them, but were secular events.

Some other EDMC events have an overtly spiritual agenda. London club Return to the Source (RTTS) was developed by Chris Decker in 1993. He drew upon his experiences while travelling, in particular the 'full moon' parties in Goa. He stated in the accompanying booklet to one of the club's albums,

> At Return To The Source it is our vision to bring back the dance ritual. A ritual is a sacred act with focused intention. Our intention is to create a modern day temple, a positive space created with love, where we can join as one tribe to journey deep into trance just as our ancestors did long ago. We view the dancefloor as a sacred space, a place to connect with our power. (Decker 1995)

A trance music scene (or subculture) developed in London, based around the Brixton venue where RTTS and another similar night, Escape From Samsara, were held, and inspired trance events throughout Britain. The EDMC trance scene has now expanded beyond this London scene and other areas where the music was popular, including Goa and Israel, to form a global phenomenon. Before RTTS events commenced, a shamanistic ritual would precede the opening of the club, and if participants took along 'tribal' instruments like drums and dijeridoos to play they would pay a reduced entry fee. Mixing images of spirituality and hedonism, Buddhism and psychedelia, world music, techno and drug culture, the club provided a model for later events.

The Boom Festival in Portugal developed more recently. Boom describes itself as

> bringing together the latest in psychedelic audio and vis-
> uals, art installations and workshops, this weeklong event
> is a harmonic convergence of people, energy, information
> and philosophies from around planet Earth and beyond . . .
> Reflecting a harmonic balance of the organic and the cyber-
> technologic, Boom 06 maps the metaphysical framework in
> accordance with Peace, Love, Unity and Repect. The tone
> is set for a transformative experience in celebration of the
> perpetual cycle of creation and re-creation – from the begin-
> ning of the whole to the Eschaton.[2]

Boom is held in a remote location in the mountains of Portugal every two years, and the journey to the venue is something of a pilgrimage. The festival is many miles from any major city and accessible only by a single road, so that the 20,000 participants have had to queue for as much as 12 hours in their cars to get from the main road to the festival site. Despite this, people come from all over the world to attend.

A bibliography on the Boom website includes texts relating to reli-gion and spirituality such as *Tao: The Watercourse Way*,[3] *Cosmic Trigger*,[4] *Supernatural*,[5] *Transfigurations*,[6] *Techgnosis*,[7] *Secret Life of Plants*[8] and *The Mysticism of Sound and Music*.[9] Some at Boom are particularly interested in such philosophy and spirituality, whereas others there have a more hedonistic philosophy of taking drugs, dancing and having fun, which is clearly also a part of the Boom philosophy, or at least its practice. Boom clearly has elements of and references to spirituality and religion.

The Synergy Project was another EDMC event that specifically engaged with issues of spirituality. It was based in London, and organ-ised monthly events that attracted several thousand people. Before its doors opened to the public, participants gathered together in a circle and held a short ritual to start off the event. The organisers aimed to create a space where clubbing could be explored in a conscious and spiritual fashion, instead of with a purely hedonistic approach. The Synergy Project mission statement described it as follows:

Synergy Project was a magical indoor festival, combining musicians, DJs, VJs, performers, and artists from all corners of creativity, joined by various proactive NGOs and charities with the expressed aim to make a difference.

In a society which generally perceives clubbing as a form of escapism associated with values of transgression, The Synergy Project re-invented the clubbing experience by transforming it into an 'educational' tool, associating healthy values of sustainability and social justice to strong role models such as respected artists and performers of the entertainment industry. Creating awareness with more efficient means to reach directly a young audience that might be otherwise reluctant to receive, respect, and incorporate such messages when proposed by conventional sources.

Offering a wide arrange alternative techniques such as Shiatsu, Reiki, Massage and Reflexology to name just a few, the healing area provided a space where people could enjoy relaxation and health/stress awareness therapy. Training workshops and information about alternative health practice and contacts with healers throughout the country are provided. Synergy also utilized a large crew of welfare staff whose primary focus is to ensure that attendees have the best possible/safest of times.[10]

The Synergy Project has developed into three separate organisations, club event Luminopolis, charity/community project The Synergy Centre and music café the InSpiral Lounge.

EDMC events involve numerous rituals. Clubbers collect before an event in homes and bars, to talk, prepare, dress, listen to music, and purchase or distribute drugs, warming up for the night ahead. Finding out about, finding and travelling to events is often difficult, with advertising via specialist media, websites or (for illegal events) carefully guarded phone numbers passed on by word of mouth or via the Internet. Queues to get into EDMC events have their own associated cultures. Dress restrictions are sometimes applied for those arriving at a club, creating a coherence of identity of the club members. Entering a club or event is a rite of entry and passage, with door security staff choosing who can come in by their own varied criteria, or searching people as they enter. Some trance clubs (such as Gatecrasher in Sheffield and Vague in Leeds) would turn away those in typical 'townie' clothing such as shirts with ties, in order to maintain the required atmosphere. Queuing rituals provide a transition from the outside world to the fantasy world within, a sense of delineation between the profane or mundane outside and the sacred or special inside. The use of the word 'club' itself implies membership and a hierarchy that features subcultural capital. Ehrenreich tells us that music/dance-based

> rituals serve to break down the sufferer's sense of isolation
> and reconnect him or her with the human community . . .
> because they encourage the experience of self-loss, that is,
> a release, however temporary, from the prison of the self,
> or at least from the anxious business of evaluating how one
> stands in the group or in the eyes of an ever-critical God.
> (Ehrenreich 2006: 152)

Entry into an event along with others with similar dress codes and behaviours is one way in which this sense of community is engendered.

Clubbers' behaviour at EDMC events echoes the behaviour of followers of mainstream religions in a number of ways. Clubbers can often be seen raising their hands up towards the light(s) in a fashion very reminiscent of a Pentecostal church service. Raising one's hands was a sign for clubbers I spoke to of release, rapture, escape, ascension and ecstasy. They reached upwards and outwards towards lights that shone above them, framing their heads like a nimbus or halo – a signifier in religious art of the sacred or divine – surrounded by heavenly smoke-machine-generated clouds. To enhance the visual experience on the dance floor, moving light is manipulated by technological lighting effects using moving mirrors, as well as by using video projection. Light is used much like religious art, to set the sacred space apart from the mundane, to create an impression of the earth and heaven meeting, bringing the divine into the present. Images from a range of religious traditions, science fiction and fantasy, on decor and video screens, add to the otherworldly effect. Club decor also often features psychedelic patterns and fluorescent colours lit with ultra-violet light.

It is clear that EDMC has elements of religion, spirituality and meaning, although Christian influences are often imbued with a sense of transgression. This is partly a reaction to the history of repression of ecstatic music and dancing practices in Europe by Christianity, particularly by Puritan and Lutheran traditions. This history has become ingrained in dualistic Western European attitudes to the body:

> Whereas Western dance forms control body movements and sexuality itself with formal rhythms and innocuous tunes, black music expresses the body, hence sexuality, with a direct physical beat and an intense, emotional sound – the sound and beat are felt rather than interpreted via a set of conventions. (Frith 1983: 19)

> Popular music has stayed especially close to 'the body' – compared to the art music of the European aristocracy and bourgeoisie – and that this intimacy has increased in the twentieth century. (Ibid.: 258)

It is in disco that we first see many of the essential elements of EDMC fully developed.

EDMC began as 1970s disco, an African American dance form, not as 1980s house as often thought. From black and Latino gay disco culture, elements of Christianity (from black/gospel church culture), African trance culture (from African American secular music culture) and 1960s psychedelia were transmitted into what became EDMC. Like its predecessors jazz, blues, rhythm and blues, rock and roll and soul house music, little known in the USA, crossed the Atlantic into British white culture, became hugely popular and eventually migrated back to the USA (Till 2007: 183–201).

The most conclusive pieces of evidence of spirituality and religion within EDMC are the innumerable accounts of transcendent experiences described by clubbers themselves. I describe these in a recent publication.[11] They recount, again and again, individual mystical experiences of transcendence and rapture. Writer Simon Reynolds relates a similar experience,

> Borne aloft in the cradling rush of sound, swirled up and away in a cloud of unknowing, for the first time I truly *grasped* what

it was to be 'lost in music'. There's a whole hour for which I can't account. (Reynolds 1998: xxvii)

However, because EDMC is sometimes perceived as an escape from life, and often involves the use of drugs, clubbers often do not recognise their activities as religious or spiritual. This does not mean necessarily that they are not spiritual. Bailey has explained how those within social institutions such as EDMC may not see their activities as religion, if this religion is implicit rather than explicit: 'It will not be seen, by the actor, as religious' (Bailey 2002: 9). Other terms will be used instead of 'religion', such as spirituality, philosophy, world view, lifestyle, way of life, ideal or identity.

The dimensions of the sacred experience and the human encounter are clearly present in EDMC, but the encounter with a traditional God is not part of the experience. Clubbers had no interest in an external organisation or deity whose opinions, obedience or control was enforced or required. Encounter is with other people and the self, although there is a sense of the infinite, the transcendental and the void, and it is partly the language, traditions and history of religion that are rejected rather than its philosophical essentials. Certainly if 'The sacred . . . is that which is special and set apart' (Bailey 2001: 78), it would seem that EDMC is sacred.

Drug taking in EDMC

The widespread taking of illegal drugs in clubs is described in some detail in numerous texts, including for example Reynolds (1998), Shapiro (1999) and Deehan and Saville (2003). The illegality of the recreational use of drugs that are commonly taken within EDMC in the UK, such as ecstasy, ketamine, cocaine and amphetamines, has created a prohibition culture similar to that of the USA in the 1920s, with the same associated gun crime, criminalisation of supply and underground chic of illegality. The rituals of finding drugs, smuggling them into clubs, taking them, discussing them and recovering from them are an important part of the ritual practice of EDMC.

Ecstasy (or MDMA) has been the most prominent and common drug taken, and the initial growth of EDMC in the UK in 1988 came at a time when the use of ecstasy became widespread. Reynolds describes ecstasy, its history and effects, very clearly (ibid.: xxiv). The initial effects of the drug can cause nervousness, discomfort, distraction, stomach aches and vomiting, and this fits in well with Rouget's (1985) descriptions of the crisis that occurs before a possession trance ritual. It is following such a crisis that possession takes place, typical symptoms being loss of time[12] and a different consciousness. Within EDMC, once a clubber has overcome their crisis, and started to feel happy and comfortable, has overcome this first period, they are described as having 'come up'. As serotonin and dopamine floods the brain, and the heartbeat is raised by fast dancing and the effects of the drug, a powerful euphoria is often experienced. This period is commonly known as 'rushing', when physical and emotion pleasure 'rushes' through the clubber.

There are a number of typical behaviours or rituals associated with having taken ecstasy, including the developing of drug distribution networks, often small scale and involving friends providing drugs for one another; sharing drugs with other people; giving and receiving massages; spending time cooling down and talking intensely to a single other person in a chill out room, bar, on the floor of a corridor or any other space; looking after other people who are struggling to cope with the effects of drugs; loss of awareness of the passing of time; and loss of memory. Drug taking was clearly a powerful ritualised process for clubbers, and it is important to note the sense of transgression and excitement granted within EDMC by illegality, by the legal and physical risks involved in taking potentially lethal unregulated narcotics.

Trance and possession

EDMC has many similarities to possession trances in some traditional cultures. As Sylvan puts it 'connections between music, rhythm, dance, and trance induction are consciously recognised by ravers, and the induction of the trance state is a specific goal of the music' (Sylvan 2005: 68). One clubber told me that 'All concept of time disappears' when clubbing having taken ecstasy. Loss of memory is an important indicator of a trance experience. Malbon describes EDMC altered states as 'oceanic experiences' (Malbon 1998: 105–33). Saunders et al. (2000) and Reynolds (1998) both discuss EDMC in terms of trance rituals and ecstatic states. Robin Sylvan regards EDMC as having taken its trance traditions from African Yoruba and Fon traditions, via African American music (Sylvan 2005: 90).

Rouget describes trance as involving movement, noise, being in company, crisis (or altered state), sensory overstimulation, amnesia and no hallucinations,[13] as well as trembling, protruding eyes and thermal disturbances (Rouget 1985: 11–14). These are typical conditions for a clubber in an ecstasy-induced EDMC altered state. Rouget defines two kinds of trance, possession and shamanic (ibid.: 23). The latter seems to most resemble what happens in EDMC, but shamanic trance usually involves the shaman making his or her own music. More similar still to EDMC is the trance culture of the African Pygmies and Bushmen, where the trance is a shamanic one, but unusually one in which the music is made for the shaman, something that is characteristic of possession trances, an unusual position between possession and shamanism (ibid.: 139–47), which is similar to that within EDMC.

Rouget describes how hallucinatory drugs are sometimes used to trigger trance (ibid.: 25), as is continuous loud drumming (ibid: 53), and how a person's character changes during a trance. He describes the crisis that precedes a trance state, the difficult transition from a normal to a trance state (ibid.: 54); how more recent initiates react more strongly and are more likely to achieve a trance state, the more experienced having more control over whether they go into a trance; and that music usually accompanies trance and is generally thought to induce it. He states that this music includes rhythmic breaks, complex rhythms, changes in stress and rhythmic irregularities, speeding up and getting louder and the musical collapse, or breakdown. Trance dancing is described as frenetic and repetitive (ibid.: 91). 'The possessees are the ones who do the dancing . . . the music is played for the purposes of dance' (ibid.: 114). 'Dancing . . . brings about modifications in the dancer's state, both at the physiological and psychological level' (ibid.: 117).

These descriptions by Rouget of elements of traditional trance are similar to what is found within EDMC. Similarly, the trance dance movements mentioned by Rouget are ones I have seen often in EDMC, and will be familiar to any clubber, 'packed one against the other, the dancers bend their knees in time with one another, accompanying each beat with a kind of pounding of the ground and a back-and-forth swaying of the body' (ibid.: 312), and 'an alternating movement consisting of swaying the entire body from right to left and left to right while the head oscillates from one side to the other' (ibid.: 312).

'Music and dance act in conjunction to produce an emotional state favourable to possession' (ibid.: 182). According to Rouget 'the universality of trance indicates that it corresponds to a psychophysiological disposition innate in human nature' (ibid.: 3). Rouget also makes it clear that throughout the world trance is usually associated with religion and ritual as well as music and dance. Ehrenreich (2006: 18) and Nettl (2000: 469) both describe this association as universal. Ehrenreich describes the history of the loss of these traditions in some detail. She also makes it clear that this kind of activity is a core part of traditional human activity.

Crisis, individualisation and ritual as social technology

Frith states that 'the musical experience has been individualised. Music is no longer a necessarily social or collective affair' (Frith 1996: 237). Trance is usually associated with a crisis. The crisis that is associated with EDMC seems to be related to the process of individualisation in society, the loss of and discomfort with traditional forms of community, religion, and ritual, and the loss of communal ritual celebration and connection. This has created what Ehrenreich describes as 'the terrible sense of psychic isolation – "the unprecedented inner loneliness" – that a competitive sink or swim economy imposed' (Max Weber 1992, quoted in Ehrenreich 2006: 143–4).

Heelas and Woodhead discuss the rise of the secondary institution within counterculture, as a response to the individualisation of society and the 'homeless self' (Woodhead and Heelas 2001: 43–4), quoting Marx, 'all that is holy is profaned' (Marx 1848/1977: 224) and Weber, 'a world once charged with religious significance had been "disenchanted" by "the tremendous cosmos of the modern economic order"' (Weber 1904–5/1985: 181). A secondary institution is a useful term for EDMC, as, unlike Christianity, they provide no 'order of things to be obeyed . . . and therefore provide much greater freedom for people to exercise autonomy' (Woodhead and Heelas 2001: 53). EDMC is a process of re-enchantment, of addressing the problem of the homeless self.

As traditional community foci in Britain have become deconstructed, clubbers have sought out new places where they feel part of a community, in which 'music becomes a focus for values as it mediates the life of a community' (Chernoff 1979: 37), and 'the collective voice is given precedence over the individual voice of the artist or composer' (Hebdige 1979: 11), art leading the re-enchantment of culture and society (Gablik 1991: 167–83). Ehrenreich describes this using Turner's term of 'communitas' (Turner 1969), 'the spontaneous love and solidarity that can arise within a community of equals' (Ehrenreich 2006: 10), as well as Durkheim's term 'collective effervescence' (ibid.: 14), 'that which leads individuals to seek ecstatic merger with the group' (ibid.). Lynch also describes Turner's 'communitas' in terms of EDMC as

> a temporary unstructured form of community in which all participants are, for a brief time, regarded as equal. This idealised form of human community offers a brief respite from the hierarchical nature of day-to-day society, and provides an important reminder of people's essential quality and of the importance of treating people with proper regard. (Lynch 2005: 30–31)

The Boom Festival and psy-trance sub-genre's mantra of PLUR (peace, love, unity and respect) are examples of EDMC actively trying to create communitas, and indeed the Boom organisation quotes Turner on their website. Sylvan associates communitas very closely with EDMC:

> Traditional rites of passage emphasize the liminal quality of this transition from adolescence to adulthood by separating the initiates from the rest of society, stripping them of their normal social identity, placing them in their own temporary form of alternative community – which Turner called *communitas* – and initiating them through a powerful encounter with the sacred. Raves do all of these things in exactly the same sequence. (Sylvan 2005: 102)

Becker points out that:

> Whereas it is the individual who experiences trancing, it is the group and the domain of coordination that triggers trancing. There must be changes in the neurophysiology of

the trancer for trancing to occur, but those changes are not attributable simply to the brain/body of a self-contained individual. They occur through the group processes of recurrent interactions between co-defined individuals in a rhythmic domain of music that is intrinsically social, visibly embodied, and profoundly cognitive. (Becker 2004: 129)

Possession trance consists of a change of identity, from an individual to a part of the group. Music puts the individual experiencing the trance in tune, in phase, in time with the rest of the group.

The music is the instrument of communication between the subject and group . . . Creates a certain emotional climate . . . leads the adept towards the spirit possessing him . . . provides the adept with the means of manifesting this identification and thus of exteriorising his trance . . . It is the only language that speaks simultaneously to the head and the legs . . . it is through music that the group provides the entranced person with a mirror in which he can read the image of his borrowed identity and to reflect this identity back again to the group in the form of dance . . . A means of reasserting the unity of the group and reinforcing awareness of that unity among all of its members. (Ibid.: 325–6)

Dancing and music allow the body to be synchronised to the time domain of the music, the external clock of the repeating bass drum, pounding at a loud level, overloading the senses and entraining the body to its rhythms. I encountered a number of clubbers whose heartbeat had become completely synchronised with the music, each heartbeat coinciding exactly with each bass drum beat. Multiple cross rhythms were being maintained in different parts of the body while dancing, triplets or syncopated semi-quaver rhythms perhaps danced by the hands, with quavers represented by bending the knees, crotchets by head movements and the torso moving swaying side to side each bar. This coordination of body and music has powerful effects, further confusing and disrupting any clear perception of a simple, normal flow of time, and locking to the beat.

The dancing physically takes the body and mind out of its usual time frame, aided by drugs and expectation. This continues for a sustained period, with beat-matched music that is designed to seem like one sustained musical stream, far from the typical Western individual three-minute pop song tradition. A large number of members of the group all take this ritual journey together, hearts synchronised and minds stilled, the dancing providing a focus for the consciousness, which can move from the brain into the body, allowing the instinct and subconscious to become stronger, freeing the participant from inhibition and individualisation. Holding hands in the air, lights and smoke whirling overhead, perception dominated and sensory inputs overloaded, carried on in the euphoria of group dynamic and with brains flooded with drug-induced dopamine and serotonin overloads, EDMC has acted much like millennium fever at the end of the twentieth century, becoming a major cultural movement. After the night's exertions, the ritual ends with small groups of exhausted participants returning to homes, 'coming down', discussing the events of the night and listening to slower music, sustaining the effects of the trance gently as the effects of the drugs slowly wear off.

Studies have shown that music may be able to lock or entrain brainwave activity to a specific frequency, and directly assist the achievement of trance states. The repetitive beats of EDMC, with its driving rhythms, high volumes, and pervasive 16th note sub-division, added to strobe and other lights flashing in time, facilitation by drug taking and participants dancing vigorously to the music, may act to drive the rhythms of body and mind in time to the music, helping the brain to slip into an altered state of consciousness or trance state (Di Paolo 1999).

According to Turow and Berger (2011), several cognitive psychologists hold that perception, attention, and expectation are all rhythmic processes subject to entrainment. In other words, even when a person is only listening to speech or music, their perceptions and expectations will be coordinated by their entrainment to what they hear. Entrainment is fundamental then, not just to coordinate with others, but even to perceive, react to, and enjoy music. Music, as an external oscillator entraining our internal oscillators, has the potential to a ect not only our sense of time but also our sense of being in the world.

Thus music takes EDMC participants away from their everyday experience and entrains them to the pulse of the music and culture surrounding them. For two rhythms to be entrained they must be coupled together. It is the common culture of electronic dance music, and the shared ecstatic experience of music and dancing, that couples people together, entraining them into community and connection.

EDMC spirituality

Lynch has identified three elements of EDMC spirituality: a deeper connection with the self, the finding of this connection through an essential non-verbal form (dancing, ritual), and the enjoyment of freer and more intimate relationships with others (Lynch 2002: 88–9). These elements combine and mix together. EDMC spirituality involves many elements including the creation of sacred spaces; the emulation of images of heaven using clouds of smoke and moving lights; out-of-body, otherworldly experiences; opposition and transgression; subcultural authority and authenticity; ecstatic journeys; ritual possession trance practices triggered by dancing, drugs and music; no reference to an external deity that has an absolute right to obedience; and the replace-ment of priests by DJs, drug dealers and promoters whose jobs are to facilitate and enhance the mystical experiences of the clubbers.

It is a democratised, postmodern, re-enchanting, reconstructive spirituality. It is autonomised, subjectivised, both individualised and rational/holistic, both individual and group/communal, emotionally intelligent and explorational, seeking sensation and ecstasy, mystical, and involves power and spiritual authority being owned, not passed or delegated. It relates to 'somethingism',[14] connection to the earth, Gaia theory, the neo-pagan, direct connection with others and God, general (rather than special) revelation, the experiential, body positivism and liberal attitudes to sexuality. It is focused on community facilitation and celebration, 'communitas' and collective effervescence. Ethical decisions within EDMC spirituality are the responsibility of the individual, in line with Zygmunt Bauman's *Postmodern Ethics*, rather than an 'absolute line of reference' (Lynch 2005: 94–5), or external power, sometimes guided by the concept of PLUR: peace, love, unity and respect.

EDMC is a significant cultural phenomenon. Figures showed in 1996 that 42 per cent of the general population of the UK visited clubs at least once a year, 43 per cent of 15–24-year-olds visited a club once a month or more often (Mintel 1996), and 1.8 per cent of 16–59-year-olds used ecstasy in 2006/7, a figure that has stayed roughly the same (between 1.5 and 2.2 per cent) since 1995 (Nicholas et al. 2006/07). These figures suggest that in any one year more people might go to a nightclub than attend a Christian church in the UK. The percentage of the UK population that is taking ecstasy (1.8 per cent) is larger than taking that part in Pentecostal (1 per cent) or Charismatic evangelical (1.2 per cent) Christian churches (Ashworth and Farthing 2007).

EDMC contains elements of spirituality, meaning and religion. As mainstream culture has become more individualised and less community orientated, and as it has lost its celebratory traditions, rituals and religions, some of the original roles of organised religions have been replaced by EDMC, which acts much like a religion. It draws upon those traditions around it in a 'pick and mix', postmodern fashion, using material from various wisdom traditions. It has adopted elements of Christianity from African American music culture, but because of their transmission through secular black music culture and gay disco, these elements are referenced in a transgressional fashion. Also transmitted through African American music traditions are trance practices that have their roots in African possession rituals, with particular similarities to Pygmy/Bushmen traditions. These trance practices are reinforced by the use of illegal drugs to cybernetically enhance the effects of the trance, and add to a sense of subcultural authority and transgression, the illegality providing a barrier to re-absorption into the mainstream and a resultant process of disenchantment and deconstruction. The crisis that this trance responds to is that of the individualisation of society, the homeless self, and the trance ritual acts to help the individual feel reconnected to or reinserted into a community. Clubbers do not see this activity as religious, but this may be because the religion is implicit rather than explicit, with clubs acting as what may be described as a secondary institution. However, EDMC acts much like a religion, providing a site of escape and transcendence, a sacred space separate from everyday existence and a key focus of community and identity.

As the traditional dominant religious Christian tradition dies away in the UK and elsewhere, many young people in particular have had no religious context in which to practice ritual together, have group mystical experiences or develop communities of like-minded belief. The fundamentality and universal human desire for such activities is shown in that EDMC in general, and the trance scene in particular, has grown to provide these functions for a large body of young people. 'Chill out' rooms provide the equivalent of prayer, meditation and spaces to meet and discuss, and the dancefloor provides a liminal space or temporary autonomous zone akin to worship, offering self-loss within the group. Music replaces thought and takes people out of normal time, and drug taking exaggerates the experience. This is a youth cult however, and it lacks sustainability, becoming less attractive as participants age or have children, who cannot generally participate. As musical trends change and shift it is uncertain whether the EDMC trance cult will continue or die out, but there remains much to consider, study and evaluate about this musical religious movement of postmodernity.

Notes

The URLs cited in the Notes and References were
correct at the time of writing.

1

Jerusalem in Uppsala

1   Biographical information on the group is taken from the group's official
    website ('Jerusalem'), unless otherwise stated.

2   I personally saw them live in Jakobstad, Finland, in 1979.

3   The website history says that they moved in 1992, but an interview in
    Trons Värld Vol. 14 (published in August 1993) talks of an upcoming
    move in September 1993. This unclear detail is discussed further below.

4   As the quote says, Jerusalem initially went to Uppsala to join the Livets
    Ord Bible school, but they stayed on to become members of the con-
    gregation. Here I do not make a distinction between the congregation
    and the school, but use the word 'congregation' as a term for the whole
    organisation.

5   The issues that trouble Livets Ord are the same as those facing many
    other religious organisations of the same type, for example issues related
    to changes in gender roles or pluralistic values. One concrete example is
    their quite extensive educational system, including their own university,
    based on the view that the Swedish school system has been 'severely
    secularised' (see the website 'LivetsOrd.se – Utbildning'). Other examples
    are discussed in this chapter.

6   It must be kept in mind that this chapter is also such a representation.

7   Another artist who played an important role particularly as a 'figurehead'
    to the outside world was the singer Carola Häggqvist (married name
    Søgaard), one-time winner of the Eurovision Song Contest, who was a
    member of the congregation during the same period as Jerusalem (see e.g.
    Magazinet 1989b: 4–7).

8   For a lengthier discussion on the coverage of music in *Trons Värld*, see
    Häger 2001.

9   For a study on the role of music and particularly worship music in a
    neopentecostal faith/prosperity congregation in Norway, see Lie 1996.

10 The album cover is reproduced on Jerusalem's website (dancing.jpg).

11 Ekman makes references to other sermons in the same collection, saying for example 'last night I spoke of . . .', which indicates the time of production. He mentions the recent election of Bill Clinton on one tape, which also gives an idea of the period when it was produced.

12 In Swedish 'församling', which also can be translated more directly as 'congregation', but here is assumed to refer to Christianity in a more general sense.

13 He did not recall the exact time at our interview in 1999, but says that he left in connection with a meeting where Ekman criticised Christian rock.

14 In Swedish 'skvala', which alludes to the term 'skvalmusik', low quality popular music or muzak.

15 The music news columns in *Trons Värld* do not mention a Scandinavium festival in 1992, but *Trons Värld* 1990b: 19 and 1991a: 14 report from the event held in those years, and do not mention Jerusalem.

16 See website 'Jerusalem – Uffes sida'.

17 According to the news section on Jerusalem's website, several songs from *Dancing on the Head of the Serpent*, including the title track, were on the set list of the concerts in the first decade of the twenty-first century.

18 The answer is not dated, but it cannot have been written earlier than 1998, since an album from that year is mentioned (see 'Jerusalem – Uffes sida').

19 *Prophet* 2004.

20 The lyrics quoted here are taken from the band's website.

21 In Swedish 'ojdå', an exclamation of surprise, and perhaps a positive one.

22 There were other indications in the late 1990s that the conflict between Livets Ord and the surrounding society was becoming less sharp. One example is the service from Livets Ord televised on Swedish public service television in January 1999 (see for example *Dagen*, 26 January 1999).

2
Christian Metal in Finland

1 For more on the concept of *scene* see Kahn-Harris 2007: 100–101.

2 Moberg 2009a: 135–8; see also Howard and Streck 1999: 5–13. It should also be noted that these 'requirements' constitute central, and constantly debated, components of the world of contemporary Christian music more generally.

3 http://fi.wikipedia.org/wiki/Kristillinen_metallimusiikki#Kristillinen_metalli_Suomessa; Moberg 2009a: 175–6.

4 Moberg 2009a: 176; http://fi.wikipedia.org/wiki/Kristillinen_metallimusi-

ikki; *Ristillinen* 2007/7, 7–29. The name 'Ristillinen' is a play on words. The word 'risti' means 'cross' in Finnish.

5 http://www.metalliunioni.com/forum/.

6 http://metallimessu.com/info/mita-metallimessu-on/.

7 Hoover 2006, 290; similar arguments are also made by Chidester 2005, 32; Lyon 2000, 56–64; and Stout 2001, 69–70.

8 http://evl.fi/EVLUutiset.nsf/Documents/0DCC039A551C3C6CC225753 20038BE6F?OpenDocument&lang=FI.

9 For example Giddens 1991; Lash 1995.

10 For example Heelas and Woodhead 2005.

3
Shout to the Lord

1 'Eldkollektivet' could be translated as 'the Fire Collective' or 'the Fire Community'. 'Gud av värme' means 'God of warmth'.

2 'Eld' means 'Fire', and is the name of a record label run by Mia Petersson, who releases the records of Eldkollektivet and a few others.

3 Kjell Lönnå is a popular Swedish singer with his own TV show.

4
Jews United and Divided by Music

1 I wish to thank Debbie Friedman, Jess Gold, Michael Shire, Steven M. Cohen and Fiona Karet for their help in researching this chapter.

2 Western Europe here includes the UK. Whilst the UK is often an exception to wider European trends, in religious terms it is within the European mainstream.

3 In January 2011, as the proofs for this book were being prepared, the news was received that Debbie Friedman had died of pneumonia at the age of 58. Although she would not have agreed with all of my arguments in this chapter, I would like to dedicate it to her memory.

4 All quotations from Debbie Friedman in this chapter are taken from a personal interview with her conducted on 5 January 2006.

5 *Tikkun Olan* is a kabbalistic concept meaning 'repair of the world'. The concept has been extremely important in the development of non-Orthodox theology in recent years.

6 Friedman played concerts at two UK synagogues in 1992 and 1997.

7 These figures are rough estimates. My thanks to Steven M. Cohen for providing me with an unpublished paper comparing findings from the 1990 and 2000 National Jewish Population Surveys.

5
The Return of Ziryab

1   According to Yusuf Islam he was even encouraged by the imam at the Central Mosque in London to continue to perform music that was of a high moral content and not offensive. But he soon came to the conclusion that he should take the 'safest position and get out'. See Alexis Petridis interview with Yusuf Islam in the *Guardian*, 11 December 2006.

2   For a description, discussion and analysis of the function of Islam and religion within youth groups using music, see, for example, Gardell 1995; Heinonen 2004; Larsson 1998, 2004; Samy Alim 2005 and Wuerth 2000.

3   This discussion of Islam and music is primarily based on a reading of Hjärpe 2001; Hammond 2005; Marcus 2007; Nelson 2001; Otterbeck 2004; Al-Qaradawi 2001 and Ramadan 1999.

4   This subject is discussed thoroughly in Nelson 2001.

5   Nelson 2001, p. us 2007; Otterbeck 2004; Al-Qaradawi 2001 and Ramadan 1999.

6   See Gräf and Skovgaard-Petersen 2009 on Yusuf al-Qaradawi.

7   Quotation from Petridis 2006; cf. Yusuf Islam 2007. See also the concert DVD, *Cat Stevens Majikat Earth Tour 1976* (released 2004). This DVD also contains an interview with Yusuf Islam in which he gives a retrospective view on his relationship with music and why he left the music industry.

8   Some of his negative experiences from the music industry are documented in the interview on the concert DVD, *Cat Stevens Majikat Earth Tour 1976* (released 2004). Another example is found in his answer to a question regarding his impressions of his meeting with Nelson Mandela and the AIDS relief concert in South Africa in 2003. He says: 'Peace Angela [the name of the person who raised the question] – It was great to be back "in-the-loop". Meeting some of the "old" faces was nice – Jimmy Cliff being one of them. But I also noticed some of the "agro" which made me give up the music biz and want to get out 25 years ago. Egos are still very much present in the echelons of power and control at such events. But the cause was well worth it.' The quotation is taken from IslamOnline. net, 'Live Dialog with Yusuf Islam', 5 December 2003.

9   See the interview on the concert DVD, *Cat Stevens Majikat Earth Tour 1976* (released 2004).

10 'Insha Allah' means 'if Allah wills'. Quotation taken from Islam 2007.

11 See Islam 2007. This opinion is even supported by the Islamic republic in Iran, which has decided that Cat Stevens's songs provide a good example for the youth. According to Yusuf Islam the opinion of the Iranian *ulama* illustrates that there could be positive aspects to some

music and arts. This information is also taken from 'Music A Question of Faith or Da'wah'. From this point of view Cat Stevens (and later on Yusuf Islam) could be seen as an acceptable alternative for Muslims (i.e. for those Muslims who have problems with Western popular culture). Many Muslim theologians are today calling for Muslim alternatives to Western popular culture. See, for example, my article on the animated movie *Muhammad: The Last Prophet* in Larsson 2006.

12 For example, the single 'Indian Ocean' was recorded in 2005 to help the victims of the tsunami catastrophe in Christmas 2004.

13 On this school, see the website http://www.islamia-pri.brent.sch.uk/about.html (printed 1 October 2007). On the importance of this night in Islamic traditions see Netton 1997.

14 See the website http://www.nightofremembrance.com/nor.htm (printed 1 August 2008). This concert has also been released as a CD/multimedia record.

15 The children's records are 'I look, I see' and 'A is for Allah' and the two edifying records are 'The Life of the Last Prophet' (which is a so-called digibook, i.e. a book and a record) and 'Prayers of the Last Prophet'. For more information on the Children's records see http://jamalrecords.com/ilookisee/ and http://www.jamalrecords.com/catalog/albums_aifa.html. Similar information can be found for the edifying records on http://www.jamalrecords.com/catalog/albums_potlp.html and http://www.mountain-oflight.co.uk/products_lotlp_db.html.

16 This statement is quoted from 'The former Cat Stevens, Yusuf Islam, to perform at Nobel Peace Prize Concert', *International Herald Tribune*, 31 October 2006.

17 In November 2007 – at the time of writing the last part of this article – this performance was possible to watch on YouTube (retrieved from www.youtube.com/watch?v=eoSidI8ldPA).

18 See IslamOnline.net, 'Live Dialog with Yusuf Islam', 5 December 2003.

19 Quotation taken from IslamOnline.net.

20 See the interview on the DVD, *Cat Stevens Majikat Earth Tour 1976* (released 2004).

21 Yusuf Islam gives a detailed description of the reactions in the interview on the DVD, *Cat Stevens Majikat Earth Tour 1976* (released 2004).

22 Yusuf Islam describes his conversion to Islam in the interview on the DVD, *Cat Stevens Majikat Earth Tour 1976* (released 2004).

23 A detailed outline of this homepage is found in Gräf 2008.

24 Asadullah 2003. On Small Kindness see http://yusufislam.org.uk/sk/mission.htm (printed 1 October 2007).

25 See 'Yusuf Islam Releases 1st Commercial Album' (14 November 2006) and 'Yusuf Islam to Release New Album' (1 October 2006), both on IslamOnline.net.

26 On Ziryab, see Farmer and Neubauer 2002: 517–18.

27 The best-known *daa'ii* is the Prophet Muhammad, whom all Muslims should try to emulate since he is the normative role model and example for all Muslims. On this concept and the related word *da'wa* (which Yusuf Islam is explicitly referring to); see, for example, Janson 2002.

6
The Meanings of the Religious Talk in French Rap Music

1 Many French journalists and researchers underline this characteristic of French rap, but this point of view is also shared by American researchers and especially Tony Mitchell (see Mitchell 2005).

2 'Popular' must here be understood in all its French significations (of/for/ by the people, the masses, well-liked, cheap, common . . .) and not only its English meaning.

3 This and all other translations from French is done by the author.

4 English: 'The Rumour'.

5 The French word is 'banlieues'. According to its social position and population, this area could be a French equivalent of the American 'inner city'.

6 'Naïf, novice mais tellement fier d'évoluer dans un système parallèle, où les valeurs de base étaient pêle-mêle *Peace, Unity Love and Having Fun*, le hip-hop n'a jamais eu besoin de gun ni de gang, de toys ni de bande mais plutôt de la foi de ceux qui en défendent la mémoire et l'éthique, les valeurs essentielles', NTM, *Tout n'est pas si facile* (Everything is not so easy), 'Paris sous les bombes' (Paris under bombing), Epic Sony, 1995.

7 Some of these band members' stage names (Akhenaton, Kheops, Kephren, Imothep) refer to Egyptian mythology and show these members' intention to introduce spirituality into their rap without referring to a specific religion.

8 The self-productions network. These artists are neither produced nor distributed by record companies and mainly have a smaller distribution than the artists who are under contract.

9 L'Affiche no. 29, November 1995, quoted in Boucher 1998: 191.

10 NAP, *La racaille sort un disque*, High Skills Records, 1996.

11 'Ce n'est pas Dieu qui n'existe pas, c'est l'être humain / Qui est incapable de le voir / Nos yeux sont aveuglés par la matière / Limités par l'espace / Ainsi que le temps / Dieu ne peut être vu qu'avec l'œil du cœur / Celui qui connaît son âme connaît son seigneur'.

12 Fonky Family, *Si Dieu veut . . . Inch' Allah* Small-Sony, 1997.

13 Monsieur R., 'J'aurais voulu vivre comme Jésus Christ', TR: 'I would have liked to live like Jesus Christ', *Mission R*, Fifty Five, 1999.

14 Afrojazz, *Afrocalypse*, Island Records, 1997.

15 Idéal J., 'Pour une poignée de dollars' (For a Handful of Dollars), *Le combat continue*, Polygram, 1998.

16 'Pour une poignée de dollars / Je me ferais tuer pour une poignée de dollars / Que ferais-tu pour une poignée de dollars? / Peut-être qu'il sera trop tard / Quand tu le sauras, connard! / Crois-tu qu'la misère dans ce monde est illusoire / Et qu'on a plaisir à voir les nôtres au parloir? / Ecoute, regarde, pour une poignée de dollars / Les jeunes du ghetto sont prêts à aller au placard / Deal, biz, braquages en temps de crise / Espèce de connard, accuse le pouvoir!'

17 'J'ai réappris à vivre / Compris les causes de notre déclin / Et quand j' regarde mon passé, j'ai failli y passer / Si j'n'avais eu l'Islam / Peut-être que j' me serais fait repasser / Ou la moitié de ma vie en prison j'aurais passé'.

18 Kery James, *Savoir & vivre ensemble*, TR: To Know/Wisdom and live together, Savoir & Tolérance/Naïve, 2004.

19 'Dans pas longtemps, ils diront aux gosses que l'oseille c'est Dieu.'

20 'L'Islam ramène l'amour.'

21 'Que Dieu te protégé.'

22 'Que Allah le préserve du châtiment.'

23 'Grand Dieu.'

24 'Dieu est le plus grand.'

25 'C'était écrit c'est pas un hasard.'

26 'Il ne peut m'arriver que ce que Dieu m'aura prescrit.'

27 'On se dit que tout est écrit.'

28 'Don de Dieu.'

29 'Merci à Dieu de m'avoir sorti de la misère.'

30 'J'prie pour la Providence.'

31 'En espérant que Dieu et ma famille vous me pardonnez.'

32 'Y'en a qu'un à qui on doit rendre des comptes.'

33 'Seul Dieu me jugera.'

34 'Nul ne sait si c'est au paradis ou en enfer qu'on ira.'

35 'Grâce à Dieu, j'surmonte les épreuves.'

36 'Si ça va pas on s'en remet à Dieu.'

37 'J'réponds à ma haine en m'disant que Dieu est grand.'

38 'La foi comme antidépresseur.'

39 'Dans les ténèbres du Mal j'veux pas sombrer.'

40 'Le malin nous charme.'

41 'Ma foi me tient en éveil.'

42 'Que Dieu me guide j'veux pas être dans l'faux.'

43 'J'aimerais être aussi croyant que mon père.'

44 In France, the CD market is largely dominated by five 'majors': Universal, EMI, Sony, Warner and BMG.

45 *Savoir et vivre ensemble.*

46 '*S'établir dans une contrée, En devenir résident, se l'approprier, Y expulser ses habitants, misérables gens, Soumis par droit de conquête et placés, Sous dépendance politique du conquérant, Quête dominatrice, A la recherche d'un Etat, Voilà le résultat, D'une puissance colonisatrice, Aidée de l'Occident.*'

47 'Tu ferais quoi si on avait tué ton père, détruit ton toit ? Je parle pour moi : ouak' Allah, J'aurais envie de faire un carnage Haine pour haine, balles perdues et plus.'

48 'Si à tes yeux on prend position, comprend bien, Qu'on parle pas en tant que musulmans Rien qu'en tant qu'êtres humains.'

49 'Les tristes héritiers de la vérité stricte.'

50 'J'suis du ghetto.'

51 'J'suis issu de la banlieue, et ça, tu peux l'sentir à cent lieux.'

52 'Depuis que tu fumes, tu n'aimes que les Colt, tu nages à ton crawl, Mets le feu à la caisse, prends ta téc pour le Pentagone, Tu ne fais qu'alimenter les stats, vandaliser les stades, Plus tu en ajoutes, plus tu fais bander les faffs'.

53 A massive demonstration by the children of first-generation immigrants.

54 Interview by Gilles Médioni, 'Les rappeurs d'Allah', *L'Express*, 7 June 2004.

55 This same idea could also explain – in a paradoxical way – that the riots in the French suburbs were expressed through violence in November 2005. The absence of a political project and of a programme of struggle for social equality led to social disorder, violence, and more deeply, to self-destructive behaviour as rioters burnt mainly the cars of the inhabitants of their own areas as well as their collective infrastructure.

56 'Que devient notre communauté? Combien se sont égarés? L'ont quittée? De ceux-là le diable s'est emparé. Qu'ils soient maudits! Mais qui est notre ennemi déclaré? Lui qui de l'Islam certains a séparé' (*La Science Une Lumière*).

57 Chronicle of Kery James's album, *Savoir et vivre ensemble*, www.lehiphop. com.

7
Why didn't the Churches Begin to Burn a Thousand Years Earlier?

1 Varg Vikernes in the radio programme *Gamle synder* ('Old Sins') on NRK P4, 1995.

2 Information taken from the source material that Torstein Grude collected in connection with his TV documentary 'Satan rir media' (1998, Subfilm, Bergen), will be referred to as 'Grude's material', and the informants will be referred to anonymously by the letters 'A', 'B', 'C' etc. Grude generously lent this source material to me while I was doing my research project on Norwegian black metal and writing my Master's thesis. The only exception to my anonymous use of Grude's informants is made for Varg Vikernes. Vikernes was one of my own core informants in my Master's project and has previously consented to be mentioned by name in connection with the subject explored in this chapter. I have not contacted Grude's informants in order to get their permission to use their statements for my purposes.

3 Unless otherwise stated, all translations from the Norwegian are by the author.

4 The hatred is here extended to encompass the presence of other non-Nordic or non-native religions and cultural expressions than merely the Judaeo-Christian. Similar statements have occurred within the Norwegian black metal scene too, where several people have found it strange or even reprehensible that no one has yet attacked and destroyed mosques alongside Christian churches.

5 It is nonetheless worth noting that the black metal scene does not only consist of youths. Many of the people who were into black metal right from the start still have a strong attachment to the scene. The same loyalty can be observed in the metal scene more generally. Although most metal enthusiasts seem to fall for this musical genre when they are quite young, the commitment to it seems to last forever in many cases. To many, metal becomes an integral part of their life, sometimes even a lifestyle of its own (Dunn and McFadyen, *Metal – A Headbanger's Journey*, DVD).

6 The *berserkr* was Norse warrior who became particularly frenzied in battle; the word is the origin of the English word 'berserk'. The *einherjr* were lone warriors who died in battle and were taken to Valhalla by valkyries.

7 The black metal worship of darkness also includes a strong fascination for weapons, primitive and medieval-looking ones in particular. Potential buyers could get hold of such weapons – for example 'around 60 cm long maces with 3.5 cm long spikes' from Euronymous' shop (*Helvete* 1992: 2). People were encouraged to buy those kinds of weapons before it was too late; that is, while it was still legal to sell them (ibid.). Some individuals made weapons for themselves and for sale and/or stole them. An acquaintance of Greven said that he was obsessed with weapons and even collected them (Grude's material).

8   This process of masculine identity formation reflects an understanding of masculinity reminiscent of the one advocated by the mythopoetic men's movement, as it revolves around a search for natural, authentic manhood. Both movements think that the revival of one's more wild side is necessary in order to achieve real manliness.

8
21st-Century Trance Cult

1   John Miller Chernoff, *African Rhythm and African Sensibility: Aesthetics and Social Action in African Musical Idioms*, (Chicago 1979).

2   Boom Festival, *Boom Festival 2006 Website*, available at http://www. boomfestival.org/afterboom06/index.html/ (accessed 10 July 2007).

3   Alan Watts, *Tao: The Watercourse Way* (Pantheon 1973).

4   Robert Anton Wilson, *Cosmic Trigger* (Rowhalt 1995).

5   Graham Hancock, *Supernatural* (Arrow Books 2006).

6   Alex Gray, *Transfigurations* (Inner Traditions 2001).

7   Erik Davis, *Techgnosis* (Three Rivers Press 1999).

8   Peter Tompkins and Christopher Bird, *Secret Life of Plants* (Harper 1989).

9   Hazrat Inayat Khan, *The Mysticism of Sound and Music* (Shambhala Publications 1996).

10   The Synergy Project, *Mission Statement*, available at http://www.thesynergyproject.org/content/view/41/105/ (accessed 2 March 2009).

11   'Possession trance ritual in electronic dance music culture: a popular ritual technology for reenchantment, addressing the crisis of the homeless self, and reinserting the individual into the community', book chapter in Deacy 2009.

12   As the participant is focused on the passing of musical time, normal time often passes unnoticed.

13   Ecstasy is defined in comparison as being characterised by immobility, silence, solitude, no crisis, sensory deprivation, recollection and no hallucinations. This perhaps corresponds more closely to the experience of clubbers when 'chilling out' after clubbing. The two are opposite poles of the same continuum.

14   'Somethingism' is an English translation of the Dutch word 'ietsisme'. Whereas agnostics are not sure what they believe, 'somethingism' reflects a belief that 'there must be something' (i.e. some kind of higher power), without a willingness to adopt any particular religion. The term was popularised in the Netherlands in newspapers and on television.

References

Introduction

Benestad, Finn, *Musik och tanke. Huvudlinjer i musikestetikens historia från antiken till vår egen tid* (Lund: Studentlitteratur, 1978/1994).

Bossius, Thomas, *Med framtiden i backspegeln. Black metal och transkulturen. Ungdomar, musik och religion i en senmodern värld* (Gothenburg: Daidalos, 2003).

Gilmour, Michael, *Call me the Seeker: Listening to religion in popular music* (New York: Continuum, 2005).

Grout, Donald, *A History of Western Music* (London: J.M. Dent & Sons, 1960/1978).

Gymnasieeleven och livsfrågorna (Stockholm: Skolöverstyrelsen, 1974).

Hjärpe, Jan, 'Islam och musik', I *Tro & tanke* 2001: 1 (Uppsala: The Research Council of the Swedish Church (Svenska kyrkans forskningsråd, 2001)).

Howard, Jay R. and Streck, John M., *Apostles of Rock: The splintered world of Contemporary Christian Music* (Lexington: The University Press of Kentucky, 1999).

Melnick, Jeffrey, *A Right to Sing the Blues: African Americans, Jews and American Popular Song* (Cambridge, MA: Harvard University Press, 2001).

Sjödin, Ulf, *Mer mellan himmel och jord? En studie av den beprövade erfarenhetens ställning bland svenska ungdomar* (Stockholm: Verbum, 2001).

Slobin, Mark, *Fiddler on the Move: Exploring the Klezmer World* (Oxford: Oxford University Press, 2000).

Spencer, Jon Michael (ed.), *Theomusicology. A Special Issue of Black Sacred Music: A Journal of Theomusicology* 8/4 (1994).

1
Jerusalem in Uppsala

Books and journals

Arnroth, Thomas, *Dina harpors buller* [The noise of thy viols] (Uppsala: Trons Värld Ordbild, 1991).

——, *Hur den kristna rocken spelade ut sin roll* [How Christian rock lost its relevance] (Uppsala: Magazinet, 1993).

Berger, Peter, *The Sacred Canopy: Elements of a Sociological Theory of Religion* (New York: Doubleday, 1967).

Berger, Peter and Luckmann, Thomas, *The Social Construction of Reality: A Treatise in the Sociology of Knowledge* (London: Penguin, 1966/1971).

Coleman, Simon, 'Livets Ord och det svenska samhället. Analys av en debatt' [Livets Ord and Swedish society. Analysis of a debate], *Tro & Tanke* 4 (1991), pp. 27–73.

Ekman, Ulf, 'Den kristna rockens bedrägliga inflytande [The devious influence of Christian rock]', *Magazinet* 4 (October 1993b).

Häger, Andreas, 'Djävulen i Österbotten. Om den österbottniska rockdebatten på 1980-talet [The devil in Ostrobotnia. About the Ostrobotnian rock debate in the 1980s]', in: Andreas Häger (ed.) *Populärkultur under press. Studier av finländska tidningstexter om populärkultur* (Vasa: Institutet för finlandssvensk samhällsforskning, 1997, pp. 153–74).

——, *Religion, rock och pluralism. En religionssociologisk studie av kristen diskurs om rockmusik* [Religion, rock and pluralism. A sociological study of Christian discourse on rock music] (Uppsala: Uppsala universitet, 2001).

Hall, Stuart (ed.), *Representation: Cultural Representations and Signifying Practices* (London: Sage, 1997).

Holmström, Krister, *Den kristnes frihet. Ledartiklar ur Trons Värld* [The freedom of a Christian. Editorials from Trons Värld] (Uppsala: Trons Värld Ordbild, 1996).

Lie, Kenneth R., *Lovsang – middel til ekstase eller en vei til Gud?* [Worship – a means for ecstasy or a way to God?] (Søreidgrend: Sigma Forlag, 1996).

Magazinet, August 1989a; September 1989b; August 1990a; October 1993a.

Noizegate Music, 'Jerusalem', 2/2005, pp. 6–11.

Trons Värld magazine 1/1988a; 7/1988b; 11/1988c; 1/1990a; 7/1990b; 8/1990c; 16/1990d; 19/1990e; 6/1991a; 19/1992a; 7/1993a; 14/1993b.

Website references

Dagen, 26 January 1999. http://www.dagen.se/arkiv/arkivartikel. asp?ID=&TextID=57610; [accessed 16 January 2004].

dancing.jpg, http://www.jerusalem.se/discography/dancing.jpg [accessed 19 January 2004].

Jerusalem, http://www.jerusalem.se [accessed 12 March 2010].

Jerusalem, – Uffes sida, http://www.jerusalem.se/swe/aktuellt/uffes.html; http://web.archive.org/web/20010611003706/; http://www.jerusalem.se/swe/aktuellt/uffes.

LivetsOrd.se – Utbildning. http://www.livetsord.se/default.aspx?id Structure=520; [accessed 19 September 2006].

Livets Ord webshop, http://webshop.livetsord.se/asp/product.asp?idp=636; [accessed 13 March 2010].

Prophet, http://www.jerusalem.se/discography/prophet.asp; 14.1.2004.

Audiovisual sources

Ekman, Ulf, *Musikens återupprättelse - din andliga tempeltjänst inför Gud* [The restoration of music – Your spiritual temple service before God] Livets Ords Kassettbibliotek UES45 (Uppsala: Livets Ord [audio tape], 1993a).

Jerusalem, *Dancing on the head of the serpent.* JMRLP 55001 (Uppsala: JM Records, 1987).

Jerusalem, *Jerusalem music video.* FRVD001 Fruit Songs [video], 2000.

Låt elden brinna. Inspelad live med Livets Ords kör [Let the fire burn. Recorded live with the Livets Ord choir]. LOVCD 17 (Uppsala: Livets Ord, 1996).

Interviews

Interview with former Livets Ord member, here nicknamed 'Håkan', conducted in 1999.

Telephone interview with *Trons Värld* chief editor Krister Holmström 27 September 1999.

2
Christian Metal in Finland

Books and journals

Bennett, Andy, *Cultures of Popular Music* (Maidenhead: Open University Press, 2001).

Brown, Charles M., 'Apocalyptic unbound. An interpretation of Christian speed/thrash metal music', in: Lundskow, George N. (ed.) *Religious Innovation in a Global Age. Essays on the Construction of Spirituality* (Jefferson, NC: McFarland & Company, 2005, pp. 117–37).

Cameron, Helen, 'The decline of the Church in England as a local membership organization: Predicting the nature of civil society in 2050', in: Davie, Grace, Heelas, Paul and Woodhead, Linda (eds) *Predicting Religion: Christian, Secular and Alternative Futures* (Hampshire: Ashgate, 2003, pp. 109–19).

Chidester, David, *Authentic Fakes: Religion and American Popular Culture* (Berkeley: University of California Press, 2005).

Clark, Lynn Schofield, 'Introduction to a forum on religion, popular music, and globalization', *Journal for the Scientific Study of Religion* 45/4 (2006), pp. 475–9.

Davie, Grace, *Religion in Britain since 1945: Believing without Belonging* (Oxford: Blackwell Publishing, 1994).

Giddens, Anthony, *Modernity and Self-Identity: Self and Society in the Late Modern Age* (Stanford: Stanford University Press, 1991).

Heelas, Paul and Seel, Benjamin, 'An ageing new age?', in: Davie, Grace, Heelas, Paul and Woodhead, Linda (eds) *Predicting Religion: Christian, Secular and Alternative Futures* (Hampshire: Ashgate, 2003, pp. 229–47).

Heelas, Paul and Woodhead, Linda, *The Spiritual Revolution: Why Religion is Giving Way to Sprirituality* (Oxford: Blackwell Publishing, 2005).

Hoover, Stewart M., *Religion in the Media Age* (New York: Routledge, 2006).

Howard, Jay R. and Streck, John M., *Apostles of Rock: The Splintered World of Contemporary Christian Music* (Lexington: Kentucky University Press, 1999).

Kahn-Harris, Keith, *Extreme Metal. Music and Culture on the Edge* (Oxford: Berg, 2007).

Kääriäinen, Kimmo, Niemelä, Kati and Ketola, Kimmo, *Religion in Finland. Decline, Change and Transformation of Finnish Religiosity*, Church Research Institute Publication 54 (Tampere: Church Research Institute, 2005).

Lash, Scott, *Reflexive Modernization: Politics, Tradition and Aesthetics in the Modern Social Order* (Chicago: University of Chicago Press, 1995).

Lynch, Gordon, *Understanding Theology and Popular Culture* (Oxford: Blackwell Publishing, 2005).

Lyon, David, *Jesus in Disneyland. Religion in Postmodern Times* (Cambridge: Polity Press, 2000).

Mahan, Jeffrey H., 'Reflections on the Past and Future of the Study of Religion and Popular Culture', in: Lynch, Gordon (ed.) *Between Sacred and Profane. Researching Religion and Popular Culture* (I.B.Tauris: 2007, pp. 47–62).

Martin, David, *On Secularisation. Towards a Revised General Theory* (Hampshire: Ashgate, 2005).

Mikkola, Teija, Niemelä Kati and Petterson, Juha, *The Questioning Mind. Faith and Values of the New Generation* (Tampere: Church Research Institute, 2007).

Moberg, Marcus, 'The internet and the construction of a transnational Christian Metal music scene', *Culture and Religion* 9/1 (2008), pp. 67–82.

Moberg, Marcus, *Faster for the Master! Exploring Issues of Religious Expression and Alternative Christian Identity within the Finnish Christian Metal Music Scene* (Diss. Åbo: Åbo Akademi University Press, 2009a).

——, 'Popular Culture and the "Darker Side" of Alternative Spirituality: The Case of Metal Music', in: Tore Ahlbäck (ed.) *Postmodern Spirituality*

(Scripta Instituti Donneriani Aboensis XXI. Åbo. The Donner Institute for Research in Religious and Cultural History, 2009b).

Neimelä, Kati, 'Nuorten aikuisten suhde kirkkoon', in: Mikkola, Teija; Niemelä, Kati and Petterson, Juha (eds) *Urbaani usko: Nuoret aikuiset, usko ja kirkko*, Kirkon Tutkimuskeskuksen julkaisuja 96 (Tampere: Kirkon Tutkimuskeskus, 2006, pp. 43–65).

Neimelä, Kati and Koivula, Annika, 'Uskonnollinen kasvatus sillanrakenta-jana', in: Mikkola, Teija; Niemelä, Kati and Petterson, Juha (eds) *Urbaani usko: Nuoret aikuiset, usko ja kirkko*, Kirkon Tutkimuskeskuksen julkaisuja 96 (Tampere: Kirkon Tutkimuskeskus, 2006, pp. 163–77).

Partridge, Christopher, *The Re-enchantment of the West (vol. 1): Understanding Popular Occulture* (London: Continuum, 2004).

——, *The Re-enchantment of the West (vol. 2): Alternative Spiritualities, Sacralization, Popular Culture and Occulture* (London: Continuum, 2005).

Ristillinen, Issue 7 (2007), pp. 7–29.

Schultze, Quentin J., 'Touched by angels and demons: religion's love-hate relationship with popular culture', in: Stout, Daniel A. and Buddenbaum, Judith M. (eds) *Religion and Popular Culture. Studies on the Interaction of Worldviews* (Ames: Iowa State University Press, 2001, pp. 39–48).

Sohlberg, Jussi, 'The esoteric milieu in Finland today', in: Tore Ahlbäck (ed.) *Western Esotericism* (Scripta Insitituti Donneriani Aboensis XX. Åbo. The Donner Institute for Research in Religious and Cultural History, 2008, pp. 204–16).

Stout, Danel A., 'Beyond culture wars: An introduction to the study of religion and popular culture', in: Stout, Daniel A. and Buddenbaum, Judith M. (eds) *Religion and Popular Culture. Studies on the Interaction of Worldviews* (Ames: Iowa State University Press, 2001, pp. 3–17).

Thompson, John J., *Raised by Wolves: The Story of Christian Rock & Roll* (Toronto: ECW Press, 2000).

Weedon, Chris, *Identity and Culture: Narratives of Difference and Belonging* (New York: Open University Press, 2004).

Website references

'Kristillinen metallimusiikki' http://fi.wikipedia.org/wiki/Kristillinen_ metallimusiikki [accessed 21 March 2009].

Kristillinen metalliunioni: http://www.metalliunioni.com/forum/ [accessed 21 March 2009].

Metallimessu: http://metallimessu.com/ [accessed 21 March 2009].

The Evangelical Lutheran Church of Finland: http://evl.fi/EVLUutiset. nsf/Documents/0DCC039A551C3C6CC22575320038BE6F?Open Document&lang=FI [accessed 21 March 2009].

3

Shout to the Lord

Books and journals

Bossius, Thomas, 'Varför ska Djävulen ha all den bra musiken? En musikhistorisk översikt över den kristna populärmusikens framväxt', in: Björnberg, Alf, Hallin, Mona, Lilliestam, Lars and Stockfelt, Ola (eds) *Frispel: Festskrift till Olle Edström* (Gothenburg: Department for Culture, Aesthetics and Media, 2005, pp. 507–28).

Croasmun, Matthew, 'Authentisch feiern mit Rockmusik. Zum Liturgieverständnis der Vineyard-Bewegung', in: *Musik und Kirche* 1 (Kassel: Bärenreiter 2005, pp. 16–20).

Evenbratt, Martin, *Frikyrkomusik – Lovsång & Vineyard* (Gothenburg: Undergraduate paper, Department of Musicology, University of Gothenburg, 2003).

Hughes, Tim, *Here I Am to Worship* (Ventura, CA: Regal Books, 2004).

Powell, Mark Allan, *Encyclopedia of Contemporary Christian Music* (Peabody, MA: Hendrickson Publishers, 2003).

Thorsén, Stig-Magnus, *Ande skön kom till mig. En musiksociologisk analys av musiken i Götene Filadelfiaförsamling* (Gothenburg: PhD dissertation, Department of Musicology, University of Gothenburg, 1980).

Webber, Robert E., *The Younger Evangelicals. Facing the Challenges of the New World* (Grand Rapids, MI: Baker Books, 2002).

Other printed sources

Cederborg, Carina, 'Den lovsjungande församlingen. Om lovsångens plats och betydelse i gudstjänsten', in *Läsaren*, the congregation paper of the Saron Church in Gothenburg, December 2003.

Cederborg, Carina and Mattson, Emil, 'Tillbedjan'. Originally published in *Läsaren*, the congregation paper of the Saron Church in Gothenburg. Here, though, taken from the home page of the worship group Manna: www.musiker.nu/manna/ord/emil_mattson.htm.

Dagen, 25 March 2003a: 'Han har lovsången som livsstil.'

——, 4 June 2003b: Lovsång är inte min stil.'

——, 10 September 2003c: 'Vi gör musik med hjärtat.'

——, 20 October 2004a: 'Som 'Allsång på Skansen' i kyrkan?'

Einarsson, Tomas, 'Review of *Såsom eld – elden kommer inifrån*', *Trots Allt* 7 (2002), p. 8.

Jaktlund, Carl-Henric, 'Review of Eldkollektivet's CD *Gud av värme*', *Gyro* 3 (2005a).

Pålsson, Benjamin, 'Review of the CD *Bara hos Dig. Live från Livets Ord – Youth*', *Gyro* 5 (2005b), p. 40.

Petersson, Lars, 'Editorial', *Lovsång* 2 (2005), p. 3.

Pilgrim, No. 2, 2001, Stockholm: Cordia.

Sandwall, Peter, Cover text of the LP *Din väg skall öppnas. Lovsång och tillbedjan – Your Way Will Be Opened. Praise and Worship*, 1981.

Thorstensson, Sara, 'Review of Hillsong United's CD *Look To You*', *Gyro* 3, 2005.

Trots Allt, No. 7, 2002.

Wallgren, Madeleine, *Höj jubel! Liten lovsångshandbok* Hästveda (Vingårdens förlag, 2000).

Zschech, Darlene, *Berörd av himlen redan här* (Värnamo: Semnos förlag, 2005).

——, *Extravagant Worship* (Bloomington, MN: Bethany House, 2002).

Website references

churchNXT's home page: www.churchnxt.se.

Hillsong Australia's home page: www.hillsong.com.

Manna's home page: www.musiker.nu/manna/ord/emil_mattson.htm.

Maranatha! Music's home page: http://store.yahoo.com/maranathaweb.

Discography

Miscellaneous, *Bara hos Dig. Live från Livets Ord – Youth* (CD, INO Records/ David Media, KLOVCD26, 2005).

Miscellaneous, *Din väg skall öppnas. Lovsång och tillbedjan* (LP, Signatur, SILP 6961, 1981).

Miscellaneous, *Öppnade ögon* (LP, PRIM, LP 570590, 1979).

Eggehorn, Ylva, *En sång, ett folk* (LP, PRIM, LP 570.291, 1976).

Jesusfolket (EP, Hemmets Härold, FM 3036, 1971).

Interviews

Interview with Carina Cederborg, 29 September 2005.

4
Jews United and Divided by Music
Books and journals

Billig, M., *Rock n Roll Jews* (London: Five Leaves Publications, 2000).

Born, G. and Hesmondhalgh, D. (eds), *Western Music and its Others: Difference, Representation and Appropriation in Music* (Berkeley: University of California Press, 2000).

Cohen, J.M., '"And the youth shall see visions": Songleading, summer camps, and identity among Reform Jewish teenagers', in: Boynton, S. and Kok, R.-M. (eds) *Musical Childhoods and the Cultures of Youth* (Middletown, CT: Wesleyan University Press, 2006, pp. 187–208).

Cohen, S.M. and Eisen, A.M., *The Jew Within: Self, Family and Community in America* (Bloomington: University of Indiana Press, 2000).

Cohen, S.M. and Kahn-Harris, K., *Beyond Belonging: The Jewish Identities of Moderately Engaged British Jews* (London: UJIA Profile Books, 2004).

Davie, G., *Europe: The Exceptional Case* (London: Darton, Longman and Todd, 2002).

DellaPergola, S., Dror, Y. et al., *Jewish People Policy Planning Institute Annual Assessment 2005: Facing a Rapidly Changing World* (Jerusalem: The Jewish People Policy Planning Institute, 2005).

Gilroy, P., *The Black Atlantic: Modernity and Double Consciousness* (London: Verso, 1993).

Gruber, R.E., *Virtually Jewish: Reinventing Jewish Culture in Europe* (Berkeley: University of California Press, 2002).

Halman, L. and Draulans, V., 'How secular is Europe?', *British Journal of Sociology* 57/2 (2006), pp. 263–88.

Hart, R. and Kafka, E., *Trends in British Synagogue Membership 1990–2005/6* (London: Board of Deputies, 2006).

Lipsitz, G., *Dangerous Crossroads: Popular Music, Postmodernism and the Poetics of Place* (London: Verso, 1994).

Melnick, Jeffrey, *A Right to Sing the Blues: African Americans, Jews and American Popular Song* (Cambridge, MA: Harvard University Press, 2001).

Mitchell, T., *Popular Music and Local Identity: Rock, Pop and Rap in Europe and Oceania* (London: Leicester University Press, 1996).

Regev, M. and Seroussi, E., *Popular Music and National Culture in Israel* (Berkeley: University of California Press, 2004).

Rogin, M., *Blackface, White Noise: Jewish Immigrants in the Melting Pot* (Berkeley: University of California Press, 1996).

Schachet-Briskin, P.H., *The Music of Reform Youth. School of Sacred Music* (New York: Hebrew Union College-Jewish Institute of Religion, 1996).

Shleifer, E., 'Current trends of liturgical music in the Ashkenazi Synagogue', *The World of Music* 37/1 (1995), pp. 59–72.

Slobin, Mark, *Fiddler on the Move: Exploring the Klezmer World* (Oxford: Oxford University Press, 2000).

Summit, J.A., *The Lord's Song in a Strange Land: Music and Identity in Contemporary Jewish Worship* (Oxford: Oxford University Press, 2000).

Taylor, T.D., *Global Pop: World Music, World Markets* (London: Routledge, 1997).

Voas, D. and Crockett, A., 'Religion in Britain: Neither believing nor belonging', *Sociology* 39/1 (2005), pp. 11–28.

5

The Return of Ziryab

Books and journals

Allievi, Stefano, 'Converts and the making of European Islam', *ISIM Newsletter* 11 (2002).

Farmer, H.G. and Neubauer, E., 'Ziryab', in: *Encyclopaedia of Islam*, Vol. XI (Leiden: Brill, 2002).

Gardell, Mattias, *Countdown to Armageddon: Minister Farrakhan and the Nation of Islam in the Latter Days* (Stockholm: 1995).

Hammond, Andrew, *Pop Culture Arab World: Media, Arts, and Lifestyle* (Santa Barbara & Oxford: ABC Clio, 2005).

Heinonen, Katariina, 'Religiositeten hos raïlyssnare', in: Häger, Andreas (ed.) *Tro, pop och kärlek* (Åbo: Åbo Akademi, Religionsvetenskapliga skrifter nr 62, 2004).

Hjärpe, Jan, 'Islam och musik', in: Helle, Christiansen et al. (eds) *Teologi och musik* (Uppsala: Svenska kyrkans forskningsråd (*Tro & Tanke* (2001) 1).

Janson, Torsten, *Invitation to Islam: A History of Da'wa* (Uppsala: Swedish Science Press, 2002).

Larsson, Göran, 'Hip hop är språket och islam är livet', in: *Kriser och förnyelse. Humanistdag-Boken nr 11* (Gothenburg: Gothenburg University, 1998).

Larsson, Göran, 'Don't believe the hype. Musik, identitet och religion', in: Häger, Andreas (ed.) *Tro, pop och kärlek* (Åbo: Åbo Akademi, Religionsvetenskapliga skrifter nr 62, 2004).

Larsson, Göran, 'Animerad film i islams tjänst', in: Larsson, Göran et al. (eds) *Religion och medier. Några perspektiv* (Lund: Studentlitteratur, 2006).

Marcus, Scott L., *Music in Egypt: Experiencing Music, Expressing Culture* (Oxford: Oxford University Press, 2007).

Nelsson, Kristina, *The Art of Reciting the Qur'an* (Cairo & New York: The American University in Cairo Press, 2001).

Netton, Ian Richard, *A Popular Dictionary of Islam* (London: Curzon Press, 1997).

Otterbeck, Jonas, '"Music as a Useless Activity": Conservative interpretations of music in Islam', in: Korpe, M. (ed.) *Shoot the Singer: Music Censorship Today* (London & New York: Yed Books, 2004).

Petridis, Alexis, 'Why I am singing again: Yusuf Islam', the *Guardian*, 11 December 2006.

Al-Qaradawi, Yusuf, *The Lawful and the Prohibited in Islam* (Cairo: El-Falah, 2001).

Ramadan, Tariq, *To be a European Muslim: A Study of Islamic Sources in the European Context* (Leicester: The Islamic Foundation, 1999).

Samy Alim, N., 'A new research agenda: Exploring the transglobal hip hop umma', in: Cooke, Miriam and Lawrence, Bruce B. (eds) *Muslim Networks from Hajj to Hop Hop* (Chapel Hill & London: The University of North Carolina Press, 2006).

Wuerth, N., 'Islam från Mars – Uttryck av islam i Marseillansk hop hop: IAM & Fonky Family', (Uppsala: Teologiska institutionen (unpublished manuscript) 2000).

Website references

Asadullah, Ali, 'Yusuf Islam Takes Stance for Peace', *IslamOnline.net* (Art & Culture section) [accessed 10 March 2003].

'The former Cat Stevens, Yusuf Islam, to perform at Nobel Peace Prize Concert', *International Herald Tribune*, 31 October 2006 (retrieved from http://www.iht.com/articles/ap/2006/10/31/europe/EU_GEN_Norway_ Norway_Nobel_Peace_Concert.php).

Hussain, Meymuna, 'Yusuf Islam: using multimedia as a medium of Da'wah', *IslamOnline.net* (Art & Culture section) [accessed 9 March 2001].

Islam, Yusuf, 'Live Dialog with Yusuf Islam'; IslamOnline.net [accessed 5 December 2003].

——, 'Music A Question of Faith or Da'wah', published online on http://www. mountainoflight.co.uk/talks.html [accessed 1 July 2007].

'Yusuf Islam Releases 1st Commercial Album', *IslamOnline.net* (News/ International), 14 November 2006.

'Yusuf Islam to Release New Album', *IslamOnline.net* (News/Europe); 1 October 2006.

Audiovisual sources

Cat Stevens Majikat Earth Tour 1976. Eagle Vision (2004).

6

The Meaning of the Religious Talk in French Rap Music

Books and journals

Bazin, Hugues, *La culture hip-hop* (Paris: Desclée de Brower, 1995).
Béthune, Christian, *Pour une esthétique du rap* (Klinckeieck, 2004).

——, 'Le rap, une esthétique hors la loi' (Paris: Autrement, 1999).

Boucher, Manuel, *Rap, expression des lascars* (Paris: L'Harmattan, 1998).

Gérôme, Guibert and Parent, Emmanuel (eds), 'Sonorités du hip-hop. Logiques globales et hexagonales', *Copyright Volume!!* (Clermont-Ferrand, Ed. Mélanie Séteun, 2005).

Goffman, Erving, *Stigmates, les usages sociaux des handicaps* (Paris: Editions de minuit, 1977).

Interview with Kery James, 'Un rappeur lance un appel au savoir-vivre', rfimusique.com, 17 May 2004.

Chronique de l'album *Savoir et Vivre ensemble*, de Kery James, see: www. lehiphop.com.

Lapassade, Georges and Rousselot, Philippe, *Le rap ou la fureur de dire* (Paris: Loris Talmart, 1998).

Mitchell, Tony, 'Sonorités du hip-hop. Logiques globales et hexagonales', in: Gérôme, Guibert and Parent, Emmanuel (eds), *Copyright Volume!* (Clermont-Ferrand: Ed. Mélanie Séteun, 2005, p. 144).

Médioni, Gilles, 'Les rappeurs d'Allah', *L'Express*, 7 June 2004.

Vicherat, Mathias, *Pour une analyse textuelle du rap français* (Paris: L'Harmattan, 2001).

Discography

Afrojazz, *Afrocalypse*, Island Records, 1997.

113, *Dans l'urgence*, Small/Sony, 2003.

Assassin, *Perles rares*, Assassin Production Hostile-EMI, 2004.

Booba, *Panthéon*, Tallac Records Universal, 2004.

Fonky Family, *Si Dieu veut . . . Inch' Allah*, Small/Sony, 1997.

IAM, *Revoir un printemps*, Delabel EMI, 2004.

Idéal J., *Le combat continue*, Polygram, 1998.

Kery James, *Savoir & vivre ensemble*, Savoir & Tolérance Naïve, 2004.

Kery James, *Si c'était à refaire*, Warner, 2001.

Monsieur R., *Mission R*, Fifty Five, 1999.

NAP, *La racaille sort un disque*, High Skills Records, 1996.

NTM, *NTM*, Small/Sony, 1998.

NTM, *Paris sous les bombes*, Epic/Sony, 1995.

Oxmo Puccino, *Cactus de Sibérie*, Delabel EMI, 2004.

Rohff, *La fierté des nôtres*, Hostile-EMI, 2004.

Sniper, *Gravé dans la roche*, East West Warner, 2003.

Svinkels, *Bons pour l'asile*, Atmosphériques, 2003.

Triptik, *TR-303*, Nocturne, 2003.

TTC, *Ceci n'est pas un disque*, Bid Dada Disque Pias, 2002.

7

Why didn't the Churches Begin to Burn a Thousand Years Earlier?

Books and journals

Alver, Bente G., 'Er fanden bedre end sit rygte? Fakta og fiktion i folkelig fortælling' I: *tradisjon* 23 (1993), pp. 1–17.

Bossius, Thomas, *Med framtiden i backspegeln. Black metal och transkulturen. Ungdomar, musik och religion i en senmodern värld* (Gothenburg: Daidalos, 2003).

Engelstad, Arne, *Interart. Gjennom epokene med litteratur, bildekunst og musikk* (Bergen: Fagbokforlaget, 2000).

——, *På tvers gjennom nasjonalromantikken* (Oslo: Gyldendal Norsk Forlag, 2001).

Eriksen, Thomas H., *Kampen om fortiden. Et essay om myter, identitet og politikk* (Oslo: Aschehoug, 1996).

Harris, Keith, 'Darkthrone is absolutely not a political band: Difference and reflexivity in the global Extreme Metal Scene', paper delivered to the July 1999 IASPM conference, Sydney (London: 1999).

Helvete, Vol. 1, 1992.

Henriksen, Jan-Olav, *På grensen til Den andre. Om teologi og postmodernitet* (Oslo: Gyldendal, 1999).

Hetherington, Kevin, *Expressions of Identity. Space, Performance, Politics* (UK: SAGE Publications, 1998).

Eriksen, Thomas Hylland, 'Kampen om fortiden. Et essay om myter, identitet og politikk', in: *Aschehoug Argument* (Oslo: Aschehoug, 1996).

Kolnar, Knut, *Det ambisiøse selv* (Trondheim: Dr. art. avhandling, Filosofisk institutt, NTNU Trondheim, 2003).

Losten, Peder, 'Ödet har skänkt mig en gåva. Brevväxling med kyrkbrännare', in: *Hundre år av rörelse. Jönköpings läns museum 1901–2001*. Småländska kulturbilder (2001), pp. 113–36.

Moynihan, Michael og Didrik Søderlind, *Lords of Chaos. The Bloody Rise of the Satanic Metal Underground* (California: Feral House, 1998).

Mørk, Gry B., *Drømmer om fortiden, minner for fremtiden. Norsk black metals norrøne orientering, 1992–1995* (Tromsø: Hovedoppgave i religionsviten-skap, Universitetet i Tromsø, 2002).

——, 'With my Art I am the Fist in the face of god. – On old-school Black Metal', in: Aagaard Petersen, Jesper (ed.) (2009) *Contemporary Religious Satanism. A Critical Anthology*. London: Ashgate

Sægrov, Jon-Arne, *Svart ungdom* (Oslo: Hovedoppgave i pedagogikk, Universitetet i Oslo, 1996).

Torgovnick, Marianna, *Primitive Passions. Men, Women and the Quest for Ecstacy* (New York: Knopf, 1996).

Witosczec, Nina, *Norske naturmytologier. Fra Edda til økofilosofi* (Oslo: Oversatt av Toril Hanssen. Pax forlag, Oslo, 1998).

Audiovisual sources

Burzum: Burzum (Innspilt: 1992/Utgitt: 1992).

Burzum: Det som engang var (I: 1992/U: 1993).

Burzum: Hvis lyset tar oss (I: 1992/U: 1994).

Burzum: Filosofem (I: ?/U: 1996).

Darkthrone: A Blaze in the Northern Sky (I: 1991/U: 1992).

Darkthrone: Panzerfaust (I: 1994/U: 1995).

Gorgoroth: Destroyer (U: 1998).

Immortal: Diabolical Fullmoon Mysticism (U: 1992).

Immortal: At the Heart of Winter (U: 1999).

Immortal: Sons of Northern Darkness (U: 2002).

Metal – A Headbanger's Journey. Produced by Sam Dunn and Scot McFadyen. (DVD Seville Pictures/Banger Productions, 4306 06051, 2005).

Interviews

Various written and oral interview material produced in connection with the dissertation in my main subject (Mørk 2002).

Written interview material collected by Torstein Grude/Piraya Film in connection with the production of the documentary *Satan rir media* (1998).

8
21st-Century Trance Cult

Ashworth, J. and Farthing, I., *Churchgoing in the UK* (Teddington: Tearfund, 2007), available at http://www.tearfund.org [accessed October 2007].

Bailey, E., *The Secular Faith Controversy: Religion in Three Dimensions* (London: 2001).

—— 'The notion of implicit religion: What it means, and does not mean', in: Bailey, E. (ed.) *The Secular Quest for Meaning in Life: Denton Papers in Implicit Religion* (New York: 2002).

Bauman, Z., *Postmodern Ethics* (Oxford: 1993).

Becker, J., *Deep Listeners: Music Emotions and Trancing* (Indiana: 2004).

Bey, H., *T.A.Z., The Temporary Autonomous Zone, Ontological Anarchy, Poetic Terrorism* (Brooklyn: 1985).

Boom Festival, *Boom Festival 2006 Website*, available at http://www.boomfestival.org/afterboom06/index.html/ [accessed 10 July 2007].

Budzynski, T., *The Clinical Guide to Sound and Light*, Brainwave entrainment to External Rhythmic Stimuli: Interdisciplinary research and clinical perspectives, Stanford University's Centre for Computer Research in Music and Acoustics (May 2006), available at http://www.stanford.edu/group/brainwaves/2006/theclinicalguidetosoundandlight.pdf [accessed 10 April 2009].

Chernoff, J.M., *African Rhythm and African Sensibility: Aesthetics and Social Action in African Musical Idioms* (Chicago: University of Chicago Press, 1979).

Clayton, Martin, Sager, Rebecca and Will, Udo, 'In time with the music: The concept of entrainment and its significance for ethnomusicology', *European Meetings in Ethnomusicology*, 11 (2005), pp. 3–142.

Davis, E., *Techgnosis* (New York: Three Rivers Press, 1999).

Deacy, Chris (ed.), *Exploring Religion and the Sacred in a Media Age* (Farnham: Ashgate, 2009).

Decker, C., *Deep Trance and Ritual Beats* [CD] (Return to the Source, 1995).

Deehan, A. and Saville, E., Home Office Research Development and Statistics Directorate, *Calculating the Risk: Recreational Drug Use among Clubbers in the South East of England* (Home Office: London, 2003).

Di Paolo, E.A., 'Chapter 9: Rhythm, entrainment and congruence in acoustically coupled agents', in: On the evolutionary and behavioral dynamics of social coordination: Models and theoretical aspects, DPhil Thesis, School of Cognitive and Computing Sciences, University of Sussex, 1999, available at: http://www.informatics.sussex.ac.uk/users/ezequiel/thesis/ch9.ps [accessed 10 April 2009].

Ehrenreich, B., *Dancing in the Streets: A History of Collective Joy* (New York: Metropolitan Books, 2006).

Frith, S., *Sound Effects* (London: Constable, 1983).

—— *Performing Rites – On the Value of Popular music* (Oxford: Oxford University Press, 1996).

Freeman, W., 'A neurobiological role of music in social bonding', in: Wallin, N.L., Merker, B., Brown, S. (eds) *The Origins of Music* (Cambridge, MA: MIT Press, 2000).

Gablik, S., *The Reenchantment of Art* (New York: Thames and Hudson, 1991).

Gauthier, F., 'Orpheus and the Underground: Raves and implicit religion – From interpretation to critique', *Implicit Religion* 8/3 (2005).

Grauer, V.A., 'Echoes of our forgotten ancestors', *The World of Music* 48/2 (2006).

Gray, A., *Transfigurations* (Rochester, VT: Inner Traditions, 2001).

Gray, J., *African Music* (London: International African Institute, 1991).

Hancock, G., *Supernatural* (London: Arrow Books, 2006).

Hebdige, D., *Subculture: The Meaning of Style* (London: Routledge, 1979).

Janata, P. and Grafton, S.T., 'Swinging in the brain: shared neural substrates for behaviours related to sequencing and music', *Nature Neuroscience* 6/7 (July 2003).

Khan, H.I., *The Mysticism of Sound and Music* (Boston: Shambhala Publications, 1996).

Leventhall, G., 'What is infrasound?', *Progress in Biophysics and Molecular Biology* 93 (2007) pp. 130–37.

Lomax, A., *Folk Song Style and Culture* (Washington, DC: American Association for the Advancement of Science, 1968).

Lynch, G., *After Religion: 'Generation X' and the Search for Meaning* (London: Darton, Longman and Todd, 2002).

——, *Understanding Theology and Popular Culture* (Oxford: Blackwell, 2005).

Lynch, G., and Badger, E., 'The mainstream Post Rave scene as a secondary institution: A British perspective', *Culture and Religion Journal* 7/1 (2006).

Malbon, B., *Clubbing: Dancing, Ecstasy and Vitality* (London: Routledge, 1998).

Marx, K., 'The Communist Manifesto', in David McLellan (ed.) *Karl Marx: Selected Writings* (Oxford: Oxford University Press, 1977, orig. published 1848).

Merker, B., 'Synchronous chorusing and human origins', in: Wallin, Nils L., Merker, Bjorn, and Brown, Steven (eds) *The Origins of Music* (Cambridge, MA: MIT Press, 2000).

Mintel (Market Intelligence International Group Ltd) *Nightclubs and Discotheques* (London: Mintel, 1996).

National Toxicology Programme, The National Institute of Environmental Health Sciences, US Department of Health and Human Services, *Infrasound: Brief Review of Toxicological Literature* (November 2001), available at http://ntp.niehs.nih.gov/ntp/htdocs/Chem_Background/ExSumPdf/Infrasound.pdf [accessed 15 April 2009].

Nettl, B., 'An ethnomusicologist contemplates musical universals', in: Wallin, Nils L., Merker, Bjorn and Brown, Steven (eds) *The Origins of Music* (Cambridge, MA: MIT Press, 2000).

Nicholas, S., Kershaw, C., and Walker, A. (eds), *Crime in England and Wales 2006/2007*, available at http://www.homeoffice.gov.uk/rds/crimeew0607.html [accessed 26 October 2007].

Redfield, J., *The Celestine Prophecy* (New York: Warner Books, 1993).

Reynolds, S., *Energy Flash: A Journey Through Rave Music and Dance Culture* (London: Picador, 1998).

——, *Disco Double Take, New York Parties Like its 1975*, available at http://www.villagevoice.com/news/0128,reynolds,26281,1.html [accessed 2 August 2007].

Rietveld, H., *This is Our House* (London: Ashgate, 1998).

Rouget, G., *Music and Trance: a Theory of the Relations between Music and Possession* (Chicago: University of Chicago Press, 1985).

St. John, G. (ed.), *Rave Culture and Religion* (Abingdon: Routledge, 2004).

Saunders, N., Saunders, A. and Pauli, M., *In Search of the Ultimate High: Spiritual Experiences Through Psychoactives* (London: Random House, 2000).

Shapiro, H., *Waiting for the Man: The Story of Drugs and Popular Music* (London: Helter Skelter Publishing, 1999).

Small, C., *Music of the Common Tongue: Survival and Celebration in African American Music* (Hanover: Wesleyan University Press, 1987).

Sylvan, R., *Trance Formation: The Spiritual and Religious Dimensions of Global Rave Culture* (Abingdon: Routledge, 2005).

Synergy Project, *Mission Statement*, available at: http://www.thesynergyproject. org/content/view/41/105/, [accessed 2 March 2009].

Thornton, S., *Club Cultures: Music Meaning and Subcultural Capital* (Cambridge: Polity Press, 1995).

Till, R., 'The Blues blueprint: The Blues in the music of the Beatles, the Rolling Stones, and Led Zeppelin', in: Wynn, N. (ed.) *Cross The Water Blues* (Jackson: University Press of Mississippi, 2007).

—— 'Possession trance ritual in electronic dance music culture: a popular ritual technology for reenchantment, addressing the crisis of the homeless self, and reinserting the individual into the community', in: Chris Deacy (ed.) *Exploring Religion and the Sacred in a Media Age* (Farnham: Ashgate, 2009).

Tompkins, P. and Bird, C., *Secret Life of Plants* (New York: Harper and Row 1989).

Turner, V., *The Ritual Process: Structure and Anti-Structure* (London: Routledge and Kegan Paul, 1969).

Turow, G., *Auditory Driving as a Ritual Technology: A Review and Analysis*, Religious Studies Honours Thesis, Stanford University (20 May 2005), available at http://www.stanford.edu/group/brainwaves/2006/ AuditoryDrivingRitualTech.pdf, [accessed 18 December 2008].

Turow, G., and Berger, G., *Musical Time and Human Behavior: Perspectives on rhythm in ritual and healing* (in publication, 2007).

Watts, A., *Tao: The Watercourse Way* (New York: Pantheon, 1973).

Weber, M., *The Protestant Ethic and the Spirit of Capitalism* (London: Routledge, 1992).

Wilson, R.A., *Cosmic Trigger* (Las Vegas: New Falcon Publications, 1995).

Woodhead, L. and Heelas, P., 'Homeless minds today?', in: Woodhead, L., Heelas, P. and Martin, D. (eds) *Peter Berger and the Study of Religion* (London: Routledge, 2001).

Index